W9-AVO-950

Israel Horovitz
TWO NEW PLAYS

Israel Horovitz

TWO NEW PLAYS

Unexpected Tenderness

and

Fighting Over Beverley

Garden City, New York

Design by Maria Chiarino

Photos of the 1994 WPA Theater production of "Unexpected Tenderness" by Carol Rosegg. Photos of the 1993 Gloucester Stage Company production of "Fighting Over Beverley" and the 1994 Gloucester Stage Company production of "Unexpected Tenderness" by Tsar Fedorsky. Photos of the 1994 Stamford Theater Works production of "Fighting Over Beverley" by Jayson Byrd.

ISBN: 1-56865-131-7

PRINTED IN THE UNITED STATES OF AMERICA

INTRODUCTION

"Fighting Over Beverley" was begun as a love letter to my wife, and ended up being, instead, a serious letter to my mother and daughters.

I started out writing a kind of valentine, thanking my wife Gillian for giving up what she did, in the name of love, when she married me, left England and moved to the United States: my home. Gillian is English. She is a world-class runner, having been both British National Marathon Record Holder, and English National Marathon Champion. She has placed #1 in the Paris Marathon, #2 in the New York Marathon, #3 in the London Marathon, etc., etc. When she moved to America, she left her friends, her family and her fair bit of fame some 3000 miles behind her.

And, like most English(wo)men abroad, she never stopped looking back. The English are never totally happy off their rainy rock. No matter how frequent their visits home to England, their appetite for things English is never really sated. With rare exception, English ex-pats never stop being recognizably English.

"Fighting Over Beverley" was first conceived as a devilishly tricky, unforgivably romantic comedy, in which the same three actors were to play their characters at age twenty (Act One), at age forty (Act Two) and at age seventy (Act Three). As first written, in Act One, a young Englishwoman (Beverley) jilts her British fiancé (Archie) and runs off to America, with a twenty-year-old Yank (Zelly). In Act Two, Beverley and Zelly and their young daughter (Cecily) visit London, where Beverley has a chance meeting with Archie. In Act Three, Archie makes a surprise visit to Gloucester, Massachusetts, to Beverley and Zelly's home, where he confronts Beverley, proclaiming, "I'm taking you home with me! He's had you for 45 years. I want the rest. Enough's enough!"

As soon as I had a completed first draft, it was obvious that only Act Three was working satisfactorily. In fact, the romantic triangle seemed to me to be only truly comic when the characters were age seventy while, at the same time, Act Three's situation presented boundless dramatic possibilities.

The latter revelation summoned me to quite another muse . . . and quite another play.

I put "Fighting Over Beverley" away for more than a year and only dragged it out again at the start of the New York Playwrights Lab's sessions in September 1991, making it my Lab project for the season. And I began writing "Fighting Over Beverley" again, this time *starting out* with Archie's visit to Gloucester. I reconceived Beverley as "a profoundly unhappy woman" on the brink of taking the single biggest step of her life . . . a step into independence. I set out to write a seriously romantic play about three vital, sexy, *dangerous* seventy-year-olds, determined to . . . (You'll read the play.)

The earliest draft of the new, improved "Fighting Over Beverley" had its first public reading at Christmastime in London at a friend's apartment . . . for an audience of three. I rewrote much of the play, in time for the New York Playwrights Lab's "retreat" in Gloucester, Labor Day 1992. A month later, the Lab had its annual festival of readings of our fifteen newly completed plays at The Joseph Papp Public Theater, and in the Spring of 1993, Julie Harris did a reading of a newly revised text at Harvard's American Repertory Theatre. The play was, finally, ready for production. Although the August 1993 world premiere of "Fighting Over Beverley" at Gloucester Stage was enormously successful, for the next several months I concentrated my energies on several film projects and the play was again shelved . . . until Fall 1994, when Elizabeth Wilson starred in "Fighting Over Beverley" in a first-rate production at Theatre Works in Stamford, Connecticut. In his *New York Times* review, critic Alvin Klein (quoting one of Beverley's lines from the play) noted, "Elizabeth Wilson's performance defines thrilling." He was correct.

Nearly five years have passed since I first starting writing "Fighting Over Beverley." I cannot yet predict the play's commercial future, but, from me to you, "Fighting Over Beverley" feels like a play that will have a long life. And this, I can tell you, is quite a good feeling. A French translation of "Fighting Over Beverley" has been done by my friend Philippe Lefebvre, who also adapted "North Shore Fish" ("l'Amour dans une usine de poissons") for France. *Quatre vraies étoiles françaises* have already expressed strong interest in playing in the Paris premiere of "Fighting Over Beverley" next season. A prominent West End producer has read the latest draft and, "subject to casting," the London premiere of "Fighting Over Beverley" is "ready to roll." As for a major New York City production, I've been told that there "isn't a great deal of commercial interest in plays about older people" (*terrible* news for "King Lear"!), so, we'll have to wait and see. For my part, "Fighting Over Beverley" has already accomplished what I'd set out to do. In two substantial productions, it has held its audience. More importantly, it has *moved* its audience . . . and, after seeing the play several times in Stamford, I can report that "Fighting Over Beverley" pleased me. And it felt complete. And so, it became time for me to move on to a "new" play.

In the Fall of 1994, "Unexpected Tenderness" was just slightly more recent than "Fighting Over Beverley." In fact, the first draft of "Unexpected Tenderness" was written sometime between my writing the second and third drafts of "Fighting Over Beverley." "Unexpected Tenderness" seems to me to be the sort of play a writer should write as his/her first play. It is a rite of passage . . . extremely personal, dark, funny and sad. However bizarre, "Unexpected Tenderness" is, more than anything else, a family play. It is also that thing that audiences seem to love and critics seem to loathe: a *memory* play. In fact, "Unexpected Tenderness" is a play I avoided writing for some thirty years. It is a story I never particularly wanted to tell.

"Unexpected Tenderness" is not, strictly speaking, the blow-by-blow story of my childhood exactly as I lived it. By no stretch of imagination, even mine, is my particular childhood stageworthy. Many lies had to be told to make "Unexpected Tenderness" work for an audience, not only to cover the truth, but to cover the boring patches. We tend to look back at life and say, "My, how it's flown by!" . . . But, we tend to live life, as we watch plays, at a snail's pace, moment by moment.

People constantly ask me if "Unexpected Tenderness" is really my life's story . . . "Was that the way it was?" (Although Mike Geller, my friend/my rabbi, walked past me as he exited the Gloucester Stage production with a whispered *"I didn't know you grew up in my house!"*) Let me say it now, once and for all time, simply and clearly: while "Unexpected Tenderness" contains some of the most dramatic moments of my particular childhood, at the very same time, it is filled to the brim with some of my very best adult lies. In the end, "Unexpected Tenderness" is partly true, partly invented. It is also coherent, organized and conclusive. This is not life. This is writing.

For many years, I have written two kinds of plays. One group I call "Plays of my Mother." The other group I call "Plays of my Father." The plays of my mother tend to be softer, gentler plays . . . such as "Today, I Am A Fountain Pen" and "Park Your Car In Harvard Yard." The plays of my father tend to be stronger, more frightening plays . . . such as "The Indian Wants The Bronx" and "The Widow's Blind Date." "Unexpected Tenderness" represents the first play I have ever written that combines both styles . . . and, not surprisingly, it is the first time in my fifty-plus years and fifty-plus produced plays that I have ever written directly about my mother and my father.

"Unexpected Tenderness," like "Fighting Over Beverley," was written within the context of the New York Playwrights Lab. The first draft was started in September 1992 and evolved quite quickly (for me), being completed by late Summer 1993 in time for the Lab's annual retreat. Subsequently, with minor revisions, the play had readings at The Joseph Papp Public Theater in New York City and, a few months later, at the John Harms Theatre in New Jersey. Audiences and actors were instantly enthusiastic about "Unexpected Tenderness." I got production offers from both regional and New York City-based theatres. For my own part, I found the play to be painful, too painful, very nearly unwatchable. Nonetheless, I set August 1994 at Gloucester Stage for its world premiere. At the same time, I accepted a production offer from the WPA Theatre in New York City. I wanted things to move quickly. "Unexpected Tenderness" was not a play with which I wanted to linger for years and years, as I had with "Fighting Over Beverley."

Prior to the Gloucester Stage premiere of "Unexpected Tenderness," the only real stumbling block I could foresee was my eighty-four-year-old mother. At the end of the day, "Unexpected Tenderness" is my mother's play, not mine. I felt that I could not possibly allow "Unexpected Tenderness" to be staged without her first reading the play and giving it her blessing. If, in fact, she'd read the play and wanted it burned, I was prepared to light the match.

My mother came to stay with Gill and me for a few days at our house in Gloucester. I gave her a newly revised draft of the script to read, midmorning, as soon as the children were out of earshot, outside playing. I explained to my mother why she was being asked to read the play and why she was being asked to make her decision about the play being staged. She said, "Don't worry about me. I'm a tough cookie. Just go ahead and do the play. I don't have to read it." To which I replied, "I love you and I want to make you happy, not unhappy. Making this play public might upset you. Please, read it and decide what you want me to do."

Gill and I left my mother alone, script spread out in front of her on the dining room table. Mama read "Unexpected Tenderness" for the first time ever, while Gill and I went for a long, long, long run by the sea. Two-and-a-half hours later, when we returned to the house, my mother wasn't quite as tough a cookie as she'd been at the time we'd left. The play had shaken her and forced her to remember some of the worst moments of her life. In the end, obviously, she wanted the play to be staged and witnessed . . . and indeed it was. But, for the next two hours, my eighty-four-year-old mother shared with my wife and me some of her deepest thoughts about life and marriage and family. Much of what she said to us was being said aloud for the first time in her long life. Within those particular two hours, my mother allowed herself to have many revelations . . . and proved herself to be a woman of great strength, profound dignity . . . and of amazing grace. She is the primary reason I love and respect women as I do. She is the sole reason I ever had the impulse, the desire or the insight with which to write either "Fighting Over Beverley" (final version) or "Unexpected Tenderness" . . . two plays that dare to share living-room and locker-room secrets that make a mockery of men. Two plays that sing and celebrate the bravery and the beauty of women.

The Boston *Globe* review of "Unexpected Tenderness" was a valentine: intelligent, emotional, supportive and, for me, totally pleasing. Gloucester Stage was SRO throughout its eight-week run. "Unexpected Tenderness" marked the thirteenth new play of mine to have its world premiere at Gloucester Stage; the third new play of mine to have its New York premiere at the WPA Theatre; and the fifth new play of mine to be directed in New York by Steve Zuckerman. The WPA Theatre's cast of "Unexpected Tenderness" was inspiring. Clive Barnes, writing in the *New York Post*, championed the play, calling it "among Horovitz's very best." Mr. Barnes had an undisputable right to make that particular statement, as he had previously reviewed some twenty-five of my plays. The WPA Theatre's audiences laughed, wept and, at the end of the evening, cheered.

There are already several productions of "Unexpected Tenderness" planned in the USA, next season. Translations are underway for Germany and Italy. And here in Paris, where "Park Your Car In Harvard Yard" ("Quelque part dans cette vie") has been on stage during four seasons and "Line" ("le ler") during twenty seasons, Jean-Claude Grumberg (author of "Dreyfuss", "l'Atelier", etc.) has just read "Unexpected Tenderness" and agreed to do the French adaptation. So, happily, it looks as though "Unexpected Tenderness" will, too, have a worldly life.

ADDENDUM: I watched very nearly every performance of "Unexpected Tenderness" during its five-week run at the WPA. Not only did I love the show, I also wanted the play out of my system. I wanted to rid myself of the demons as quickly as possible and move on. Four months have passed since "Unexpected Tenderness" first opened in New York and I am midway through the first draft of a new play, "The Barking Sharks." *La lutte continue.*

Israel Horovitz
Paris, France
January 1995

Unexpected Tenderness

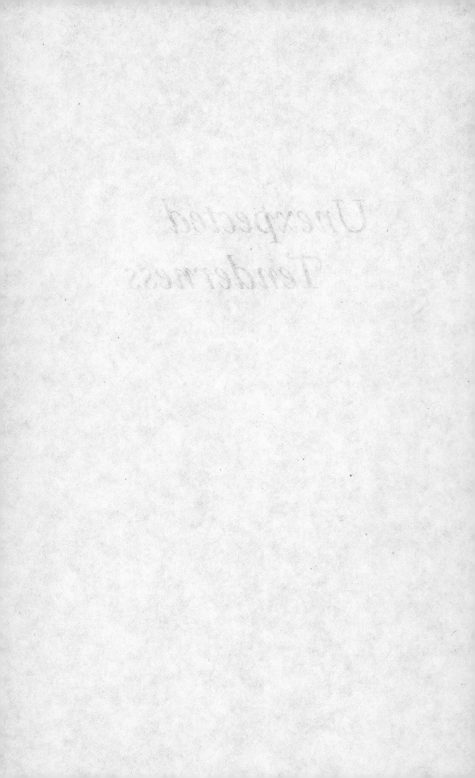

"Unexpected Tenderness" had its world premiere at the Gloucester Stage Company in Gloucester, Massachusetts on August 19, 1994. It was directed by Grey Johnson. The set was designed by Charles F. Morgan, the lighting by John Ambrosone, the costumes by Jane Stein. The stage manager was James Conway. The cast was as follows:

Roddy Stern (the Elder)/Archie Stern . . . . . . Will LeBow
Roddy Stern (the Younger) . . . . Ben Webster, David Rich
Molly Stern . . . . Paula Plum
Sylvie Stern . . . . Jessica Semeraro
Haddie Stern . . . . Patricia Pellows
Jacob Stern . . . . Barry Zaslove
Willie . . . . Mick Verga

It opened in New York City on October 16, 1994 at the WPA Theatre. It was directed by Steve Zuckerman. The set was designed by Edward T. Gianfrancesco, the lighting by Richard Winkler, the costumes by Mimi Maxmen and the sound by Aural Fixation. The production stage manager was Mark Cole. The cast was as follows:

Roddy Stern (the Elder)/Archie Stern . . . . . . Steve Ryan
Roddy Stern (the Younger) . . . . . Jonathan Marc Sherman
Molly Stern . . . . Caitlin Clarke
Sylvie Stern . . . . Karen Goberman
Haddie Stern . . . . Scotty Bloch
Jacob Stern . . . . Sol Frieder
Willie . . . . Paul O'Brien

The People of the Play

ARCHIE STERN, late thirties, handsome, strong, sad-eyed, suspicious. NOTE: Same actor plays Roddy (The Elder) throughout play

MOLLY STERN, Archie's wife; slightly younger than Archie; small, full-breasted, strikingly beautiful

SYLVIE STERN, Archie and Molly's daughter; fifteen, skinny, sad-eyed, pretty

RODDY (The Younger) STERN, Archie and Molly's son; fourteen, small, skinny, an easy smile. (NOTE: Could be played by slightly older actor, age twenty to twenty-five)

HADDIE STERN, Archie's mother; nearly seventy; small, strong-backed, plump

JACOB STERN, Archie's father; same age as Haddie; has severe Parkinson's disease; slurred speech; cannot walk unassisted

WILLIE, Archie's helper, forty; vaguely dapper

The Place of the Play

Kitchen of Stern family home, small town New England.

The Time of the Play

Early 1950s; Eisenhower is in.

A note on the accent. If possible, a North Shore Massachusetts accent ("Pahk Yo'r Cah In Hav'id Yahd") should be used by all, but for Haddie and Jacob, who should speak with a accent that is a blend of Eastern Europe and Western Massachusetts.

The first draft of UNEXPECTED TENDERNESS was written in The New York Playwrights Lab.

To My Mother

Mary, Mary,
Quite contrary,
How does your garden grow?

With brittle Shells
And broken Bells,
And one magnificent Fame Lily.

ACT ONE

ACT ONE

Scene One

Music in: Chopin on piano, lightly, sweetly.

Soft white light fades up on Roddy (the Elder) Stern center stage. He is in his late thirties; wears clothing of a truck driver (matching gray chino pants and shirt, work boots, etc.). He is handsome, sturdy, strong.

A second spotlight fades up on Roddy (the Younger), standing on staircase, facing audience.

RODDY (THE ELDER): For the past few months, I wake during the night, two or three times, every night, and I hear voices in the kitchen. It's my mother and my father. I hear them bickering mostly . . . but sometimes they laugh and, when their laughter stops, I know that they're kissing.

RODDY (THE YOUNGER) (*smiling at audience; speaks*): Each time, just before their voices go silent, they take turns yelling up the stairs for me to get ready for school.

MOLLY'S VOICE (*off*): Roddy! You'll be late for school!

(*Roddy [the Elder] turns, yells. NOTE: He is now playing Archie*)

ARCHIE: Do you hear what your mother's saying, you?

(*He switches back to playing Roddy [the Elder], without hesitation . . . or explanation to audience*)

RODDY (THE ELDER): When I give in to my curiosity and go downstairs, the kitchen's empty, of course, and I'm filled with despair.

MOLLY'S VOICE (*off*): Roddy! You'll be late for school!

(*Roddy [the Elder] yells upstairs. He is, again, playing Archie*)

ARCHIE: It's six-thirty, you! Are you quitting school?! (*No reply*) Do you hear me? I am asking you a question: Are you quitting school?!

(*Archie turns, faces audience again; smiles. He is now, once again, playing Roddy [the Elder]*)

RODDY (THE ELDER): Oh, there's something I should warn you about. I'll be playing Archie, my father—like I just did there, when I yelled. The boy who's playing Roddy (me, young) will sometimes talk to you, directly, when I'm too busy playing Archie to stop and explain things.

RODDY (THE YOUNGER) (*smiling at audience; speaks*): This confusion of father and son might be a bit disquieting at first, just like the confusion of father and son is in life. (*Nods to Roddy [the Elder]*) Okay?

RODDY (THE ELDER) (*nodding "okay"; smiles at audience*): You're clever. You'll get used to it.

(*Suddenly, Roddy [the Younger] runs upstairs, Roddy [the Elder] moves to bottom of staircase and yells up. He is once again playing Archie*)

ARCHIE: Excuse me! Am I talking to myself here?

(*Lights widen to reveal the kitchen in Archie and Molly Stern's modest apartment. The dining table is set for breakfast. Sylvie, the daughter, fifteen, sits at upright piano, practicing Chopin étude. Sylvie is dark-haired, sad-eyed, skinny, pretty. She wears a Girl Scout uniform; many merit badges.*

Archie, standing at bottom of staircase, yells upstairs again)

ARCHIE: Do you not hear me? I have to be back on the road in one half hour, precisely! . . . Willie's waiting in the truck! Do I not deserve to have breakfast with my family? Do you think I'm a stupid person, or what?

(*Roddy [the Younger], Archie's 14-year-old son, yells down stairs*)

RODDY (THE YOUNGER) (*off*): I'm up! I'm up!

ARCHIE: Yuh, right! So's Mrs. Woolf!

RODDY (THE YOUNGER) (*off*): Who's Mrs. Woolf?

ARCHIE: Your teacher's not Mrs. Woolf?

RODDY (THE YOUNGER) (*off*): My teacher's Mrs. Foxx!

SYLVIE: His teacher's Mrs. Foxx.

MOLLY (*off*): His teacher's Mrs. Foxx.

(*Molly enters from bedroom upstairs. She is slightly younger than Archie, small, large-breasted, strikingly beautiful; wears robe belted tightly at waist. She takes command*)

MOLLY: The toaster popped! Sylvie! The toaster popped! . . . Are you a *deaf person?*

SYLVIE (*stopping piano-playing*): Okay, fine, I'm getting it!

(*Sylvie goes to toaster, places toast on plate; goes to stove, begins scrambling eggs. Molly busily prepares family breakfast; sets table, pours coffee, etc.*)

MOLLY (*to Archie*): Why isn't he up?

ARCHIE: He's up.

MOLLY: How do you know?

ARCHIE: Because he's talking. He said the words "I'm up" twice. I heard him. If he weren't talking and I didn't hear him, it would be a different story. (*Eyes Molly's robe*) Close your robe tighter.

MOLLY (*tightening belt on robe; yells up stairs to Roddy*): Are you really up, you? (*No reply*) Roddy!

RODDY (THE YOUNGER) (*off*): I'm really up! I'm really up! I'm practicing my speech for the Red Feather Oratory Contest!

ARCHIE: Now we both heard him. He's really up. He said he's practicing his Red Feather speech.

MOLLY: Friday, he said he was practicing his speech for the Red Feather Oratory Contest and, forty-five minutes later, I went upstairs . . . still in bed . . .

ARCHIE: You told me . . .

MOLLY: . . . sound asleep.

ARCHIE: You told me this.

MOLLY (*screaming up staircase*): If you're not downstairs by the time I count twenty-five, there will be no Red Feather Oratory Contest, no bicycle, no skating, no YMCA and definitely no Buzzy Levine! . . . One! . . . Two! . . . (*Brings coffee to Archie*) . . . Three! . . . Four! . . . Five! . . . (*They kiss. Molly breaks from kiss; yells upstairs to Roddy*) *Ten!*

(*Lights crossfade with Archie, as he steps forward into spotlight; talks to audience as Roddy [the Elder]*)

RODDY (THE ELDER): Oh, I know what you're thinking . . . "sweet, nice little family . . . ethnic comedy . . . New Englandy . . ." If I could rewrite it and make it sweet and nice, I would have done just that . . . many years ago!

(*Suddenly, Roddy [the Elder] turns upstage, screams at Sylvie who has prepared a breakfast tray. He is now, again, playing Archie. Molly resumes meal preparation*)

ARCHIE: What do you think you're doing with that?

SYLVIE: Bringing Willie's breakfast out to him.

ARCHIE (*enraged, he moves upstage to kitchen*): Jesus! Stop, you! . . . Stop!

SYLVIE: Why? I did it yesterday!

ARCHIE: That was yesterday. I . . . said . . . "Stop"!

SYLVIE (*skidding to a stop*): Okay. I stopped.

ARCHIE (*to Molly*): Did you see her? Did you see your daughter? Did you see where she was going? (*To Sylvie*) If I ever —EVER—see you near that one alone, you'll pack your bags.

SYLVIE: I won't ever, Daddy.

ARCHIE: You're goddam right you won't ever! Gimme that!

(*Sylvie hands breakfast tray to Archie*)

SYLVIE: Here, Daddy.

ARCHIE: Where's his coffee?

SYLVIE: In the thermos bottle. I'll get it.

(*Sylvie finds thermos, hands it to Archie who tucks it under his arm, carries tray to door*)

ARCHIE: I'll be right back.

(*Archie goes to door, stops, turns to Sylvie*)

ARCHIE: It's a good thing I asked you, isn't it? (*Exits*)

SYLVIE (*after a pause; to the world*): I never get anything right for him!

MOLLY: Did you finish your Chopin?

SYLVIE: I finished my Chopin.

MOLLY (*looking at table*): No *napkins?* Are we eating like *Irish* people?

SYLVIE: I thought I put napkins on the table.

(*Sylvie gets napkins from counter; puts them on table*)

MOLLY: Did you brush your hair?

SYLVIE: I think I did.

MOLLY: Brush it again.

SYLVIE: But I really think I brushed it already!

MOLLY: Either put a sign on your head that says, "I think I brushed it already" or, go brush it!

SYLVIE: Both of you hate me!

(*Sylvie runs up stairs. Molly completes the counting*)

MOLLY: Twenty-two! . . . Twenty-three! . . . Twenty-four! . . .

(*Roddy [the Younger] runs downstairs and into room. He is 14-years old; dark-eyed, small, skinny*)

RODDY (THE YOUNGER) (*radio announcer's voice*): And once again, ladies and gentlemen, Rodney Stern is saved by the click of his Schick!

(*Molly slaps Roddy's hand twice*)

MOLLY: This is for your being late and this is for your Mr. Wiseguy mouth!

RODDY (THE YOUNGER): Thank you.

(*Jacob enters with Haddie. He is nearly seventy; has severe Parkinson's disease. He walks forward, she walks backwards. It is almost as if they are dancing. When Jacob talks, his words blur*)

HADDIE: Doesn't he look better?

MOLLY: Much better.

JACOB: I . . . d-d-d-don't!

HADDIE: You do!

MOLLY: Say "hello" to your grandmother.

RODDY (THE YOUNGER): Hullo, Grandma.

HADDIE: Hello, Roddy. Did you sleep?

RODDY (THE YOUNGER): I slept.

MOLLY: And not your grandfather?

RODDY (THE YOUNGER): Hullo, Grandpa.

HADDIE: Doesn't Grandpa look much better?

RODDY (THE YOUNGER): I guess.

HADDIE: Look at his color.

RODDIE (THE YOUNGER): That's nice, Grandpa.

(*Haddie and Jacob have negotiated a crossing of the kitchen and now attempt to negotiate a seating*)

HADDIE: Chair!

MOLLY: Chair!

(*Roddy grabs chair, pulls it back from the table. Haddie seems to be dumping Jacob on to the floor. At the last possible second, Roddy [the Younger] places the chair under Jacob's bottom, and he is seated. This is a well-rehearsed, often-performed Stern family acrobatic act*)

HADDIE: You're comfortable?

JACOB: N-n-no.

HADDIE: Why not? What's to be uncomfortable about? It's your chair! It's your family!

RODDY (THE YOUNGER): Do you want your cushion, Grandpa?

MOLLY (*passing by en route to pantry*): Hasn't he got his cushion?

HADDIE: He's got his cushion . . . he wants his newspaper . . . I'll get your newspaper.

(*Haddie exits into back room; out back door. Jacob looks at Roddy [the Younger] furtively*)

JACOB: T-t-take . . .

RODDY (THE YOUNGER): Take your cushion away?

JACOB: Y-y-yes.

(*Roddy [the Younger] tries to extricate cushion from under Jacob's bottom, but cannot manage the move*)

RODDY (THE YOUNGER): Can you kinda hop up a little, grandpa?

(*Jacob tries, but his hops get him nowhere*)

MOLLY (*re-entering from pantry; en route to table*): What are you doing to your grandfather, you?

RODDY (THE YOUNGER): His cushion's bothering him.

MOLLY: Take it out from under him.

RODDY (THE YOUNGER): I'm trying to.

(*Archie appears at window, peeking inside at his family discreetly, mysteriously. Roddy [the Younger] sees him. After a moment's pause, Archie disappears from window*)

RODDY (THE YOUNGER): He's coming back inside!

MOLLY: He's coming back inside!

JACOB: He's c-c-c-c . . .

MOLLY: *Shhhhh!*

(*Archie re-enters from outside*)

ARCHIE: Willie's sick . . . I'll have to take him to the doctor.

MOLLY: What's the matter?

ARCHIE: He's sick. He's got a sickness.

MOLLY: Should he be out there in a cold truck?

ARCHIE: He's not coming in here!

MOLLY: I'm not suggesting anything!

ARCHIE: I won't be able to eat.

(*Archie goes to Molly, kisses her lightly. He pats her bottom, lets his hand linger and rub*)

ARCHIE: I'll call you. (*Looks at her robe*) Aren't you getting dressed today?

MOLLY: As soon as they leave for school.

ARCHIE: I don't want to leave you not dressed.

MOLLY: So, wait.

ARCHIE: I can't wait. I've got to go.

MOLLY: As soon as they go to school, I'll get dressed.

ARCHIE: I don't like you traipsing around in front of everybody in a bathrobe.

MOLLY: What everybody? There's you, me, your mother, your father, our children! I'll get dressed as soon as they go to school.

ARCHIE: Fine.

JACOB: T-t-t-take . . .

RODDY (THE YOUNGER): You're gonna hav'ta hop, Grandpa!

(*Roddy [the Younger] tries again to extricate the cushion from under Jacob. Archie sees*)

ARCHIE: What are you doing to your grandfather?

RODDY (THE YOUNGER): I'm trying to get his cushion out.

ARCHIE: Leave it! He needs his cushion for comfort!

RODDY (THE YOUNGER): But, it's making him uncomfortable!

ARCHIE: Who says?

RODDY (THE YOUNGER): He says!

ARCHIE: He said that?

RODDY (THE YOUNGER): He did!

JACOB: *I* d-d-d . . .

ARCHIE: So, take it out from under him.

RODDY (THE YOUNGER): I'm trying to!

ARCHIE: I'm leaving, now.

MOLLY: Kiss your father.

(*Archie offers his cheek to Roddy [the Younger] to kiss, who does*)

RODDY (THE YOUNGER): Aren't you eating breakfast with us?

ARCHIE: Willie's sick.

JACOB (*managing to shift his position in chair; smiles with relief*): Ahhhh! B-b-b-better! Th-th-th . . .

RODDY (THE YOUNGER): You're welcome, Grandpa . . . (*To Archie*) Are you leaving, right now?

ARCHIE: Right now. Why?

RODDY (THE YOUNGER): I was kind of hoping I could try out my speech on you.

ARCHIE: Now?

RODDY (THE YOUNGER): I was kind of hoping so.

ARCHIE: I can't, now. Willie's sick.

(*Haddie re-enters from back door, carrying newspaper*)

HADDIE: Here. Your paper. I froze getting it.

(*Without pause, she goes to Jacob, lifts him by his collar, scoots cushion out from under him; puts newspaper in his hands*)

JACOB: D-d-d-don't m-m-move m-m-me! . . . *Dammit!*

HADDIE: What are you complaining about, you?

RODDY (THE YOUNGER): I think he was comfortable with the cushion under him.

HADDIE: What does *he* know? (*To Archie, as she crosses to pantry*) Why is your coat on?

ARCHIE: I have to leave early.

HADDIE: Why are you leaving early?

ARCHIE: Willie's sick.

HADDIE: I'm not surprised. (*Exits into pantry*)

RODDY (THE YOUNGER): Do you think you could help me with my Red Feather speech, Grandpa?

JACOB: N-n-now?

RODDY (THE YOUNGER): Well . . . soon.

JACOB: A-a-ask your g-g-grandm-m-mother.

RODDY (THE YOUNGER): Grandma, can Grandpa help me with my Red Feather speech?

HADDIE (*re-entering from pantry*): Aren't you making yourself late for school?

RODDY (THE YOUNGER): Why? What time is it?

HADDIE: Nearly seven-thirty. You shouldn't be speaking now. You should be eating now.

(*Suddenly, Molly screams at Roddy [the Younger]*)

MOLLY: Nearly seven-thirty, you, and still no socks on?

RODDY (THE YOUNGER): I couldn't find any socks.

MOLLY: So, instead of looking and finding them, you're going to school with no socks?

RODDY (THE YOUNGER): You were screaming at me to come downstairs!

MOLLY: No socks, like an *Italian*? (*Screams up staircase to Sylvie*) Sylvie!

SYLVIE: What? What is it? What?

MOLLY: Come downstairs, you, and kiss your father goodbye!

SYLVIE (*off*): Did you already eat without me?

MOLLY: Nobody ate anything! Your father's leaving early! Come downstairs and kiss him goodbye! (*To Roddy*) There are clean socks in the airing cupboard! Put them on.

RODDY (THE YOUNGER): What color?

MOLLY: Blue or brown, either color.

(*Roddy exits, loping up staircase; Molly screams up to Sylvie*)

MOLLY: Your father is waiting to be kissed!

RODDY (THE YOUNGER) (*off*): You just sent me up for socks!

MOLLY: I am talking to your sister!

ARCHIE: She doesn't have to, if she doesn't want to.

MOLLY: What are you saying, you?

(*Molly moves to bottom of staircase, screams upstairs*)

MOLLY: What is taking you?

RODDY (THE YOUNGER) (*off*): Me or her?

MOLLY: Her!

SYLVIE (*from staircase*): I was on the toilet! (*Enters room; goes to Archie; kisses Archie's cheek*) Why are you leaving before we eat breakfast?

ARCHIE: I've got to do something.

SYLVIE: In my whole life, you never missed eating breakfast with me before, not once, not ever! . . .

ARCHIE: I never eat with you on weekends . . .

SYLVIE: Schooldays, I mean schooldays . . . .

ARCHIE: I have to do something.

SYLVIE: What?

MOLLY: Don't pester your father!

(*Roddy [the Younger] enters carrying two pairs of socks: one red pair and one green pair*)

RODDY (THE YOUNGER): There's no brown or blue, only red and green, and they smell bad.

MOLLY: Did you get those from the airing cupboard or the hamper?

RODDY (THE YOUNGER): The hamper.

MOLLY: I said the airing cupboard!

RODDY (THE YOUNGER): I wasn't listening.

ARCHIE: Give me a kiss. I'm going.

SYLVIE: I just kissed you!

ARCHIE: Him. I'm talking to him. (*To Roddy [the Younger]*) Will you hurry, please?

RODDY (THE YOUNGER) (*kissing Archie's cheek again*): Bye, Daddy. I hope you don't hit traffic.

ARCHIE: What smells bad?

RODDY (THE YOUNGER): It's my socks. I got the wrong color.

MOLLY: Your son took dirty socks from the hamper.

RODDY (THE YOUNGER): *Dirty!?* Oh, God! I *thought* they smelled funny! I'll put them back.

(*Roddy [the Younger] runs upstairs, as Archie goes to Haddie; kisses her cheek*)

ARCHIE: Bye, Ma . . . I'm goin'.

HADDIE: Goodbye, Arthur. I hope you don't hit traffic.

(*Archie goes to Jacob; touches his bald head affectionately. Jacob looks at Archie disapprovingly. Archie withdraws his hand, kisses his father's cheek*)

ARCHIE: Bye, Pop.

JACOB: B-b-bye . . . I h-h-h-hope . . .

ARCHIE: The traffic will be fine, Pop . . . (*To everyone*) Well . . .

(*Suddenly there is a knocking on the door. We can see the figure of a man through the curtains over door's windowpane. Everyone turns, stares, seems startled. No one moves or speaks*)

WILLIE (*off*): Arch?

ARCHIE (*breaking the in-house silence*): I'm coming right out, Willie! . . .

WILLIE (*off*): I'm really feeling wickid sick, Arch.

ARCHIE: Go back to the truck! I'll come right out!

WILLIE: It must be the Virus-X! I'm feeling really punk.

ARCHIE: Go back to the truck!

WILLIE (*off*): Can you make it snappy, Arch? I'm really feeling *terrible!*

ARCHIE: I said I'm coming, didn't I? Go back to the truck!

WILLIE (*off*): Okay, Arch, sorry . . . I hate ta bother you when you're with your family and all . . .

ARCHIE (*yelling*): When you're back in the truck, I'll come out! Not before!

(*There is a pause*)

WILLIE (*off*): Okay, Arch . . . I'm goin'.

(*After a moment's pause, Archie speaks to his silent family*)

ARCHIE: I'd better start out.

RODDY (THE YOUNGER) (*re-entering, from stairs*): Who was that at the door?

SYLVIE (*whispering*): Willie.

RODDY (THE YOUNGER): Oh.

ARCHIE: I'm starting out.

MOLLY: Kiss your father.

RODDY (THE YOUNGER): I did, already!

MOLLY: Kiss him, again!

(*Roddy kisses Archie's cheek, no hug*)

RODDY (THE YOUNGER): Bye, Daddy.

(*Sylvie kisses Archie's cheek, no hug*)

SYLVIE: Bye, Daddy.

ARCHIE (*to Molly*): So?

(*Molly kisses Archie full on the lips, big hug, moderate groping*)

ARCHIE: Are you going out today?

MOLLY: Nothing special.

ARCHIE: You're sure on this?

MOLLY: I'm sure.

ARCHIE: Expecting any visitors?

MOLLY: Will you *please*?

ARCHIE: Yes or no.

MOLLY: Arthur . . .

ARCHIE: Yes or no!?

MOLLY: Arthur!

ARCHIE: *Yes or no?!*

MOLLY: No!

(*There is a pause*)

ARCHIE: It's Monday.

MOLLY: So it's Monday.

ARCHIE: Your mah-jongg group isn't playing here?

MOLLY: My mah-jongg group isn't Mondays.

ARCHIE: So when is it, then?

MOLLY: Tuesdays.

ARCHIE: Fine. I'm starting out. (*Looks at Molly threateningly*) I'll call you in an hour.

(*We hear three toots on the truck's horn*)

ARCHIE: Bastard! (*Awkwardly*) Well . . . I'm off.

(*Archie goes to door, opens it, disappears outside. Five count. Archie re-enters room*)

ARCHIE: It's raining. I need my slicker.

(*He grabs his raincoat from coat-tree, goes to door, pauses*)

ARCHIE: Well . . . I'm off, again.

(*Archie exits. There is a small silence . . . five count . . . and then Molly takes full command*)

MOLLY (*to Roddy [the Younger]*): You! Tie your shoes! (*To Sylvie*) You! Pull up your knee socks! (*To both*) Both of you! Eat your breakfast! You are not being late for school, again! Eat! (*Flashes looks at Haddie and Jacob*)

HADDIE: We're eating!

JACOB: W-w-w-we're ee-ee-ee . . .

MOLLY: Not you! Them!

(*Archie re-appears at downstairs window, peering in from outside*)

SYLVIE: Daddy, Mama.

(*Molly sneaks a peek at Archie . . . sees him, looks away quickly*)

MOLLY: Oh God! Smile, please!

(*Molly looks at her children and smiles her happiest smile. The children join in, as do the grandparents. The entire family is now smiling and eating breakfast happily . . . like a picture-book family. It's all for the benefit of Archie who spies on them*)

MOLLY (*to Haddie*): Your son will put me in my grave!

HADDIE: I hate to say it, but . . .

MOLLY: Don't say it then!

HADDIE: I have to say it!

MOLLY: So say it.

HADDIE: My son is crazy.

JACOB (*trying to yell at Archie in window*): G-g-g-get awa-awa-awa . . .

MOLLY: Don't let him see you looking! HADDIE: Don't let him see you looking!

JACOB: F-f-f-fine.

(*We hear three toots again on the truck's horn. Archie scowls, turns, exits from window*)

RODDY (THE YOUNGER): He's gone.

MOLLY: Don't let him see you looking!

RODDY (THE YOUNGER): He's gone!

MOLLY: Come sit, you! Eat your breakfast!

(Roddy [the Younger] sits, joins family meal. Molly smiles at them all)

MOLLY: Now, please, may we have ten consecutive seconds of sitting and eating in peace?

(Archie re-appears in downstairs den window, peering into his own house, discreetly spying on his family. He is framed in window as if on a giant TV screen. Sylvie is the first to notice Archie)

SYLVIE: Daddy! . . . (*Whispers*) He's back, Mama.

MOLLY (*whispering*): I see him.

RODDY (THE YOUNGER) (*whispering*): He's back!

MOLLY (*whispering*): I see him.

SYLVIE (*whispering*): She sees him.

JACOB (*full voice*): Ar-ar-ar . . .

ALL EXCEPT JACOB: She sees him!

(All begin eating animatedly, enthusiastically, as though Archie is not in the window.

After a moment, Molly covers her eyes, bows her head. Lights dim in kitchen. Roddy [the Younger] stands, moves from table into spotlight downstage. Roddy [the Younger] talks to audience)

RODDY (THE YOUNGER): My father never left for work easily. He was always certain that what he called "visitors" would be sneaking into our house as soon as he was gone. Because he drove his own truck, he was able to drive by the house several times a day and pop in . . . just to check on things. We never knew exactly what kind of "visitors" he expected to find in our house . . . earthlings or aliens. Only *he* knew for sure. And we never knew exactly what purpose the visitors would have in our particular house. What we did know, however, was not to be frightened when a man almost always appeared, peeking in through one of the ground-floor windows, shortly after our father left for work . . . or shortly before our father got home from work. The fact is, it was kind of a shock the first time I had a sleep-over at Sal Cataldo's house and his father, Mr. Cataldo, went straight to work and never once showed up in any of the downstairs windows. I also noticed that Sal and his father, Mr. Cataldo, both Italians, wore socks. And Mrs. Cataldo (who told me she was Irish before she got married) *used a napkin!*

(*Music in: A romantic 1940s tune, sung by Sinatra or Crosby. Lights fade up in kitchen behind Roddy [the Younger]. We see: Molly and Archie slow-dancing, cheek to cheek, sensually, romantically.*

Roddy [the Younger] looks into kitchen, watches his parents dance for a moment. Then, he smiles at audience)

RODDY (THE YOUNGER): Things weren't always totally crazy between my mother and father. Sometimes their romance was delicious. They loved to dance cheek to cheek. Most of all, they loved to dance cheek to cheek *at home* . . . in the *kitchen* . . . after Grandma and Grandpa and Sylvie and I had gone to sleep. Sylvie and I would lie in our beds and hear Sinatra or Crosby crooning . . . and my mother and father giggling.

(*Archie and Molly giggle . . . kiss passionately. Light fades out in kitchen. Roddy talks to audience*)

RODDY (THE YOUNGER): I'd better get to school. I'm going to practice my Red Feather speech in front of Mrs. Foxx today. I'm competing in the Red Feather Oratory Contest at school. "We have nothing to fear but fear itself." . . . That's the name of my speech. I didn't pick it. It was given to me by Mrs. Foxx. It's a quote from Franklin Delano Roosevelt. (*Simply*) Franklin Delano Roosevelt was a crippled president who hated Jews.

(*Lights fade to black.*)

ACT ONE

Scene Two

Music in: A simple Chopin piano piece, simply played. Lights fade up in kitchen an hour later. Molly, still wearing robe, sits at piano, playing.

Haddie shuttles between table to sink, bringing dishes from table. Jacob sits in his chair, newspaper on lap, asleep.

HADDIE: If your husband catches you playing the piano, he'll be furious!

MOLLY: He won't catch me. (*She plays*) It's a waste of good money to pay for lessons for one child when, for the same money, the mother, if she's clever and she pays attention, can learn to play the piano, also. (*She plays*)

HADDIE: If he comes back and catches you playing the piano, there will be hell to pay.

MOLLY: He won't catch me. (*She plays*)

HADDIE: I won't protect you.

MOLLY: Fine. (*Stops playing*) Are you happier?

HADDIE: I'm ecstatic.

MOLLY: Good. I'm glad.

(*Molly goes to sink, dries dishes*)

MOLLY: Don't forget we're going out in a while.

HADDIE: When?

MOLLY: In a while.

HADDIE: Where?

MOLLY: Hmm?

HADDIE: Where are you going?

MOLLY: Where am *I* going?

HADDIE: That's what I asked: where are you going?

MOLLY: Out.

HADDIE: Alone?

MOLLY: Excuse me?

HADDIE: Are you going out alone? (*Molly turns, looks at Haddie annoyed. Haddie explains herself*) If your husband comes home and you're out and I don't know exactly where or with who . . .

MOLLY (*slipping in correction*): . . . with whom . . .

HADDIE: . . . with *whom*, there will be trouble. And I personally couldn't give a fig where you're going or with whom, but you can understand my demanding an answer, yes?

MOLLY: Did you wash this cup?

HADDIE: You certainly didn't.

MOLLY: It's filthy.

HADDIE: I think it's fine. If you think it's filthy, wash it again.

(*Molly places cup in wastebasket*)

HADDIE: You threw the cup away?

MOLLY: It was filthy. If you don't want me to throw it away, take it out of the wastebasket and wash it.

HADDIE: It's a perfectly good cup.

MOLLY: The decision is yours to make.

(*Haddie goes to wastebasket, retrieves cup*)

HADDIE: It's not filthy.

MOLLY: Filthy.

HADDIE: It's a little soiled.

MOLLY: Drink from it, you'll be a little *diseased.*

HADDIE: Fine. (*Washes cup*) You're not going to tell me?

MOLLY: I'm going swimming.

HADDIE: In this weather?

MOLLY: Yes, in this weather.

HADDIE: You want me to tell your husband you went swimming in this weather?

MOLLY: You wanna tell him I went swimming in *different* weather?

HADDIE: And with who?

MOLLY: With *whom.*

HADDIE: I hate that.

MOLLY: It's the object of a preposition.

HADDIE: I just hate that.

MOLLY: How do you expect the children in this house to speak English correctly, if the adults in this house don't speak English correctly?

HADDIE: They're your children. You want them to spend their lives worrying about propositions [sic.], this is your business. I'm just the grandmother.

MOLLY: Fine.

HADDIE: You didn't tell me with who.

MOLLY: With whom.

HADDIE (*annoyed*): Fine. You didn't tell me with whom.

MOLLY: With you.

HADDIE: What are you giving me?

MOLLY: This is Monday. This is the day you and I are using the free trial passes they sent us for the new "Y" pool.

HADDIE: I forgot.

MOLLY: I only told you ten times.

HADDIE: I forgot. Next time, tell me twelve times! I'm an old lady. Shoot me.

MOLLY: You found your bathing suit?

HADDIE: I don't know.

MOLLY: You don't know if you found your bathing suit?

HADDIE: That is not it.

MOLLY: What is it?

HADDIE (*after a thoughtful pause*): I don't know.

MOLLY: What don't you know?

HADDIE (*discreetly, so that Jacob doesn't overhear*): I don't know if I can parade around in a bathing suit at a YMCA, you know, in front of people.

MOLLY (*discreetly, a harsh whisper*): Stay in the water. Don't parade. It's not a parading pool, it's a swimming pool.

HADDIE: Where am I supposed to put him while I'm swimming?

MOLLY: They have a crèche with a full-time babysitter.

HADDIE: I'm supposed to leave him with children?

MOLLY: For a half hour! He can read his paper.

HADDIE: I don't know.

MOLLY: What don't you know, now?

HADDIE (*nodding to Jacob*): I've never undressed in front of him.

MOLLY: In front of who? . . . whom?

HADDIE: Your father-in-law. You see what I'm saying? If I've never undressed in front of your father-in-law, how can I undress in front of the world?

MOLLY (*shocked; facing Haddie directly*): Wait a minute, wait a minute, wait a minute! You've never undressed in front of your *husband?*

HADDIE: I change in the closet.

MOLLY: Wait a minute, wait a minute, wait a minute! You change in the closet?

HADDIE: None of this is anybody's business!

MOLLY: You change in the closet?

HADDIE: I think men and women should do things privately.

MOLLY: Does he change in the closet too?

HADDIE: Not any more. The man can't even walk by himself. If I put him in the closet, I couldn't leave him in there alone! . . . He'd suffocate!

MOLLY: So you change him, and then you go into the closet and change yourself?

HADDIE: Approximately.

MOLLY: My Goddd!

HADDIE: This is nobody's business.

MOLLY: Did your mother change in the closet?

HADDIE: With me?

MOLLY: That never occurred to me. Did she?

HADDIE: Of course not! Why would my mother change in the closet with me?

MOLLY: I don't know. Why would you change in the closet by yourself?

HADDIE: Because it's private!

MOLLY: Couldn't you change in the bathroom?

HADDIE: I'm done talking on this subject.

MOLLY: Wait a minute, wait a minute, wait a minute, wait a minute! If your husband can't move on his own, why can't you just leave him somewhere where he can't see you and then change? Why do you have to go into the closet?

HADDIE: This is really none of your business. (*Pauses*) For one thing, I have to go in the closet anyway to get my nightgown. And in the morning . . .

MOLLY: Your clothes are in the closet.

HADDIE: Exactly.

MOLLY (*smiling*): So, he's never seen you naked?

HADDIE: This is nobody's business.

MOLLY: Not even once?

HADDIE: Once or twice.

MOLLY: On purpose or by accident?

HADDIE: I won't dignify a question like that.

MOLLY: Fine.

(*The women continue their housework wordlessly for a few moments*)

MOLLY: "Once or twice"? . . . That's all?

HADDIE: I suppose you just change in the open?

MOLLY: He's your son. What do you think?

HADDIE: I couldn't begin to guess.

(*Molly considers what she's just learned about Haddie. She begins to laugh aloud, quite joyously*)

MOLLY: This is really *something!*

(*Haddie looks at Molly, deeply annoyed. Molly, with some difficulty, stops laughing*)

MOLLY: How many years have you and Pa been living with us now? Ten? Twelve?

HADDIE: Five.

MOLLY: That's all?

HADDIE: Five.

MOLLY: It seems like more.

HADDIE: Five.

MOLLY: It's seems like ten.

(*Haddie suddenly screams at Jacob*)

HADDIE: Have you been listening to everything? Have you been faking sleep and listening?

(*Jacob laughs*)

HADDIE: You are disgusting!

JACOB (*enraged*): M-m-m-m-*meee?* I-I-I-*I'm* dis-g-g-g . . . ?

(*Archie appears outside kitchen window, peering in, spying on Molly discreetly, mysteriously*)

MOLLY (*seeing Archie*): Oh, God! He's back! Don't turn around!

HADDIE (*sneaking a discreet peek*): He must have forgotten something.

MOLLY: He's driving me crazy!

HADDIE: For you, crazy is not a long drive.

(*Archie disappears from window*)

MOLLY: He's coming in!

HADDIE (*to Jacob*): Don't you tell him anything that we said, you!

JACOB: W-w-w-w-would I-I-I t-t-t . . . ?

HADDIE: Shush, you!

(*Archie enters kitchen. He play-acts not seeing anybody downstairs; yells upstairs*)

ARCHIE: I'm hoooommmme!

MOLLY: What are you yelling upstairs for? We're all right here.

ARCHIE: Oh. I didn't see you in here.

MOLLY: Something wrong?

ARCHIE: Uh-uh. Why?

MOLLY: Truck troubles?

ARCHIE: Truck's fine.

HADDIE: Your wife's probably wondering why you're not working.

ARCHIE: Stay out of this, Ma!

HADDIE: Don't start in, Arthur!

ARCHIE (*white-faced anger*): Stay out of this!

JACOB: D-d-d-d-on't s-s-s-s . . .

ARCHIE: I want you in your bedroom!

JACOB: Ar-ar-ar-ar . . .

ARCHIE: I want to talk to my wife . . . alone!

(*Haddie shoots a look at Molly*)

MOLLY: It's okay, Ma.

HADDIE: Sometimes I feel like I don't know my own son.

ARCHIE: Fine.

(*Haddie goes to Jacob*)

HADDIE: Your son is banishing us from the room.

JACOB: I-I-I d-d-don't . . .

HADDIE: Shah, you! Grab ahold.

(*Haddie lifts Jacob, "dances" him backwards into bedroom.*

There is a moment's silence after they leave the room. Molly looks at Archie . . . bravely)

MOLLY: Let's have it.

ARCHIE: Is that a fresh mouth?

MOLLY (*after a pause*): No.

ARCHIE: I was riding with Willie up near the Stoneham line. He's sitting dead quiet. I ask him, "What's up with the quiet?" . . . He goes, "Ah you know, Arch . . . I'm feeling really sick with this virus-X and all." I say nothing on this. Then, no prompting from me, he goes "Molly's looking wickid good these days, Arch." I am stunned. (*Pauses, as if he's dropped a bombshell*) "Molly's looking wickid good these days, Arch." Hmmmm? (*Pauses*) I think this through for about a minute and then I put the pieces together. (*Archie walks around Molly in a circle, wordlessly, staring at her . . . looking her over*) Who are you meeting?

MOLLY: Excuse me?

ARCHIE: Who are you meeting means "Who are you meeting?" . . . That's English I'm speaking, yes?

MOLLY: Meeting where, Arthur?

ARCHIE: That's another thing I don't know. I don't know "who" and I don't know "where."

MOLLY: I'm not going anywhere and I'm not meeting anybody.

ARCHIE: Excuse me?

MOLLY: I'm not going anywhere and I'm not meeting anybody.

ARCHIE (*screaming*): I will not put up with this in my own house! I am working like a trojan, for what? So I can go off with a derelect maniac in a truck and you can have meetings? Meetings? Do you think I'm stupid? (*No reply*) Answer me! I asked you a question . . . answer me!

MOLLY (*quietly; holding back tears*): What's your question, Arthur?

ARCHIE: Do you think I'm stupid?

MOLLY (*tears betraying her courage*): No, Arthur, I don't think you're stupid.

ARCHIE (*suddenly yelling to bedroom door*): Get in here! (*No reply*) I said "Get in here"!

HADDIE (*entering from bedroom, head down, alone*): What?

ARCHIE: Where was she planning to go?

HADDIE: What are you asking me, you?

ARCHIE: Nobody speaks English in this house? Where was she planning to go?

HADDIE: Where was who planning to go, Arthur?

ARCHIE: My wife: where did my wife tell you she's planning to go?

HADDIE: She didn't tell me she was planning to go anywhere, Arthur.

ARCHIE: Oh, but she did . . . Mother.

HADDIE: Swimming.

ARCHIE: Excuse me?

HADDIE: Swimming. Your wife is planning to go swimming.

ARCHIE (*turning to face Molly*): Swimming? You're going swimming? How interesting. (*Pauses*) In the lake?

MOLLY: In the new pool at the YMCA . . . with your mother.

HADDIE (*to Archie*) I hadn't definitely agreed to go! (*To Molly*) I didn't say yes, definitely!

MOLLY: Fine.

ARCHIE: I don't think so.

MOLLY: Fine.

ARCHIE: Fine, in what sense?

MOLLY: I won't go. I'll stay home.

ARCHIE: All day?

MOLLY: All day.

ARCHIE: You promise me this?

MOLLY: Yes.

(*There is a substantial pause in which Molly looks down at her shoes, silently seething, on the brink of tears. Archie stares at her a moment, then he stares at Haddie who loses her courage and looks down. Archie laughs. He now goes to the piano, checks it over*)

ARCHIE: Was anybody playing the piano in here? (*No reply*) I asked a simple question.

MOLLY: No.

ARCHIE: No, what?

MOLLY: Nobody was playing the piano in here.

ARCHIE (*to Haddie*): You agree?

HADDIE (*after a small hesitation*): No.

ARCHIE: No, what?

HADDIE: No, nobody was playing the piano in here.

ARCHIE: Really?

JACOB (*screaming from downstairs bedroom, off*): She's l-l-*lying!*

(*Molly and Haddie wince, exchange a conspiratorial glance*)

ARCHIE (*smiling*): How interesting. (*We hear: three beeps of the truck's horn, off*) Willie. The sex fiend's got ants in his pants. (*Looks at watch*) I have to go. We're already an hour late with this load. If the mill closes for lunch before I get there, I'll be stuck in the truck with him for two extra hours. (*Goes to door; turns to Molly*) We'll talk more about this piano-playing later. (*Stares a moment silently*) I hope you're planning to put some clothes on today.

(*Archie turns to the door again, turns back, looks at both women, then turns to door a final time, exits. There is a pause. Then Archie appears at window, staring inside at his mother and his wife*)

MOLLY: Did God create men to curse women?

(*The women exchange another glance, then exit together straight upstage, arm in arm. The lights crossfade to . . .*)

ACT ONE

Scene Three

Spotlight on Sylvie, sitting at piano. Music in: Chopin piece, played by Sylvie.

Roddy (the Younger) practices his speech, more or less for Sylvie's benefit.

RODDY (THE YOUNGER): "We have nothing to fear but fear itself." That famous quotation from President Franklin Delano Roosevelt may not make a lot of sense now, but it made great sense to over a hundred million Americans just a decade ago, when this great nation was plunged into war with Hitler and many, many other maniacs . . . (*Sylvie turns, faces Roddy with a look that says she is somewhat disgusted by his attempt. Roddy turns from Sylvie, upset. He sees his own reflection in the wall-mirror, goes to it, starts over*) "We have nothing to fear but fear itself." Just a decade ago, when this great Nation was plunged into War with Hitler and many, many other maniacs, Franklin Delano Roosevelt spoke that famous quotation as he led America into a war to save the Jews, even though President Roosevelt personally hated the very Jews he was saving! (*He pauses, himself disgusted by this attempt. He moves to mirror, nose to nose with his own reflection, starts over*) "We have nothing to fear but fear itself." That famous quotation was spoken by President Franklin Delano

Roosevelt as he and many, many other Jew-hating maniacs plunged this great nation into war! . . . (*He pauses, totally disgusted by this fresh attempt, kicks chair, rolls eyes to heaven*) Shit! (*Sylvie stops playing piano, turns to Roddy, in the middle of a private thought, picking up conversation from sometime earlier*)

SYLVIE: And you're really, honestly not frightened of him?

RODDY (THE YOUNGER) (*turning upstage*): Of Daddy? Am I not frightened of Daddy?

SYLVIE: No, of President Eisenhower!

RODDY (THE YOUNGER): Why should I be frightened of President Eisenhower?

SYLVIE: That was a joke, you *derr!*

RODDY (THE YOUNGER): Did you have the dream again?

SYLVIE: Last night and the night before.

(*Light shifts to spot on Roddy. He speaks directly to audience*)

RODDY (THE YOUNGER): Sylvie has this dream all the time, in which my father wears a Nazi uniform around the house and keeps asking if anybody's seen any Jewish girls hiding in the attic.

(*Lights restore*)

SYLVIE: Last night, I killed him.

RODDY (THE YOUNGER): You killed Daddy?!

SYLVIE (*stopping playing piano*): *Shhhhh!*

RODDY (THE YOUNGER) (*whispering*): You killed Daddy?

SYLVIE: Not really!

RODDY (THE YOUNGER): I know that.

SYLVIE: I mean in my dream!

RODDY (THE YOUNGER): I know that!

SYLVIE: I had a machine gun and troops.

RODDY (THE YOUNGER): What kind of troops?

SYLVIE: Troops. Men . . . soldiers . . . working for me. He came upstairs looking for young Jewish girls and he spotted me, ya know, reading in my bed . . . and he started goose-stepping and yelling really scary things in German . . .

RODDY (THE YOUNGER): And you killed him?

SYLVIE: I gave the order and the troops killed him.

RODDY (THE YOUNGER): What about your machine gun?

SYLVIE (*looking up; weeping*): After he was dead, I shot him again.

RODDY (THE YOUNGER): How many times?

SYLVIE: . . . A lot.

RODDY (THE YOUNGER): A *lot?* (*Whistles*) Jesus, Sylvie. Jesus. (*Pauses*) You really think you ever would?

SYLVIE (*weeping*): Don't ask me that!

RODDY (THE YOUNGER): Well, you know, I'm really curious, that's all. I mean, if he came at me in a Nazi uniform and all, goose-stepping . . . speaking scary things in German

. . . (*Pauses*) Jesus, Sylvie, I'm glad it's you having the dream, insteada me. (*Pauses*) You wanna take a walk downtown with me?

SYLVIE: Uh-uh. I want to practice for a while before they come home.

(*Sylvie turns to piano, plays. Lights crossfade to . . .*)

ACT ONE

Scene Four

Spotlight on Roddy (the Elder), on staircase. He speaks to audience directly.

RODDY (THE ELDER): When I look back over my childhood, there are many, many high points to remember. . . . Humming "God Bless America" in my bathtub, under soapy water, for forty-seven seconds and not dying! . . . Getting Pesky and Williams to autograph mint-condition rookie cards in the same season! . . . Homering against Lincoln School with two men on! . . . The Red Feather Oratory Contest. . . . "We have nothing to fear but fear itself." . . . But most of all, I remember the day when my father and I rode in his green '51 Chevy flatbed truck together down to the Congo Church, where he pulled my sister Sylvie out of her Girl Scout meeting by her hair in front of the whole troop, plus a bunch of visiting Boy Scouts.

(*Lights shift to Roddy [the Younger], downstage. He takes over narration; speaks to audience, directly*)

RODDY (THE YOUNGER): Sylvie was thirteen and my father thought she had done something really bad with her friend Robert Dutton who Sylvie had promised my father she'd never talk to again a week after my father had caught Sylvie and Robert kissing on the sun porch.

(*Lights switch suddenly to Roddy [the Elder]*, now playing Archie.

Archie faces Sylvie, who sits on piano stool, center, sobbing. Archie paces in circles around the girl, railing at her. Haddie stands behind Jacob, who sits in his chair upstage left. Molly stands at sink. All watch silently, sadly)

ARCHIE (*enraged*): Marcus Rosenman's daughter went to Girl Scout camp for two months . . . FOR TWO MONTHS! . . . Do you know what happened to her? *Do you know what happened to her?* (*No reply*) I asked you a question, young lady, and I am not hearing an answer!

SYLVIE (*sobbing*): What's your question, Daddy?

ARCHIE: Do you know what happened to Esther Rosenman?

SYLVIE: I don't know, Daddy.

ARCHIE: I'm sure you don't. Do you know what "prostitute" means?

HADDIE: Arthur! JACOB: D-d-d-d . . . MOLLY: Stop, you!

SYLVIE: I don't know what that means.

ARCHIE: Oh, please, will you? Do you think I'm stupid? (*Sylvie sobs*) I asked you a question!

SYLVIE (*sobbing*): I don't know what "prostitute" means, Daddy! I don't! I really don't! I just know it's a really bad thing!

RODDY (THE YOUNGER) (*to audience*): At this point, my mother has usually had enough. She will step between my father and my sister and take control. After a moment, when it looks like my mother and father will finally kill each other, I will step in, get myself clobbered . . . but, I will defuse the bomb.

ARCHIE: The thing I hate more than a young girl's looseness is a young girl's lying! . . . And you are lying to me!

SYLVIE: I'm not!

(*Archie pulls Sylvie roughly downstage; slams her down in kitchen chair; screaming . . .*)

ARCHIE: You are lying to me!

SYLVIE: I'm not lying to you, Daddy! I'm not!

ARCHIE: Don't talk back to me, you!

(*Archie raises his hand, threatening to slap Sylvie who winces and sobs. Suddenly Molly approaches Archie with an extremely impressive bread knife in her right hand*)

MOLLY: That's enough, you! You shut that mouth now, you!

HADDIE: Molly! JACOB: D-d-d-d . . . SYLVIE: Mama, nooo!

ARCHIE: What's this, you?

MOLLY: You stay back from her! You're a crazy person!

ARCHIE: *I'm* a crazy person?

MOLLY: You heard me!

ARCHIE: I'm not the one with a bread knife in my hand!

MOLLY: You've got a bread knife for a *tongue*, you! Humiliating your daughter in front of her friends! Hurting her! Calling her names like I've never heard in my life!

ARCHIE: You want a daughter like Marcus and Ruth Rosenman's daughter, fine, that's you, but that's not me, sister! I would rather be dead than live to see such a thing! Believe me, I know where your daughter learns to make secret meetings.

MOLLY: What "secret meetings"?

ARCHIE: Hah!

MOLLY: She was at a Girl Scout meeting . . . with girls!

ARCHIE: Those were not boys there, too? Those were girls dressed up like boys?

MOLLY: They were Boy Scouts!

SYLVIE: They were Boy Scouts, Daddy!

MOLLY: It was a co-ed meeting . . . to make bird-houses!

SYLVIE: We were making birdhouses, Daddy.

ARCHIE: That wasn't Robert Dutton there next to you, who you promised me—PROMISED ME!—you would never talk to again as long as you live?!

SYLVIE (*sobbing*): I didn't know he was going to be there, Daddy! I didn't know any of the Boy Scouts were going to be there!

ARCHIE: He was next to you! You and he were laughing!

SYLVIE: He told me a joke!

ARCHIE: I'll bet he did! (*His anger is building quickly*) *I'll bet he did!* (*Archie is now violent; hand in the air, threatening Sylvie*) *I'LL BET HE DID!*

MOLLY (*moving in between Archie and Sylvie, bread knife firmly clenched in her hand*): Back, you! Get back!

HADDIE: Molly! JACOB: D-d-d-d . . . SYLVIE: Mama, nooo!

ARCHIE: Come on . . . Come ONNNN!

(*Archie now raises his fist toward Molly threateningly. Roddy [the Younger] looks at audience, shrugs, then suddenly runs straight at his father*)

RODDY (THE YOUNGER): Get away from her! Get away from her! Get away from her!

(*Roddy [the Younger] shoves Archie backwards against the table*)

HADDIE: Roddy! JACOB: D-d-d-d . . . MOLLY: Roddy, nooo!

ARCHIE: Are you out of your mind, you?

(*Roddy [the Younger] shoves Archie again. Archie slaps the boy violently. Roddy [the Younger] flies backwards, squeals; rushes at Archie again*)

RODDY (THE YOUNGER): God damn you! God damn you! God damn you!

(*Archie laughs; suddenly he violently backhands the boy, who flies backwards*)

SYLVIE: Daddy, don't!

HADDIE: Roddy! JACOB: Roddy! . . . MOLLY: Roddy!

(*There is a moment of stunned silence*)

ARCHIE (*moving to Haddie*): He hit me first. I just had a physical reaction. . . . He hit me and I hit him back. It was a *physical reaction!* (*To Molly*) I didn't want to hit him, but he hit me first, and I just hit him back. (*Goes to Roddy, tries to help him up. Roddy pulls away; moves downstage*) Get up. Roddy, get up. I'm sorry. I said it: I'm sorry. Now come on, get up. Get up!

RODDY (THE YOUNGER) (*to audience*): At this point, my father will break down and sob, uncontrollably, begging everybody's forgiveness.

(*Suddenly, Archie starts to sob. His sobbing is enormous. His body heaves, racked with sorrow*)

ARCHIE: I'm sorry I get so mad. It's just that . . . oh God, what is *wrong* with me?! I'm sorry. I apologize to everybody. I can't stop myself. I'm sorry. I am . . .

RODDY (THE YOUNGER) (*to audience*): And Sylvie, instead of ordering her troops to fire . . .

(*Suddenly Sylvie runs into Archie's arms, hugging him*)

SYLVIE: Don't cry, Daddy! It's okay, Daddy! It's okay, Daddy! Don't cry, Daddy! Don't cry, Daddy! It's really okay.

ARCHIE (*to Haddie*): I'm sorry, Mama . . . I get so mad all the time. I get so mad. I'm sorry, Mama . . . I'm sorry, Mama . . . I am.

HADDIE (*consoling Archie*): It's fine, Arthur. No harm done. It's fine. It's fine, Arthur. It's fine. It's fine.

ARCHIE (*to Jacob*): What's the matter with me, Pa? Am I a crazy person who can't control his temper? I'm so sorry, Pa.

JACOB (*reaching out; taking Archie's hand*): It's o-k-k-k-k . . .

ARCHIE: Don't stop loving me, please, Molly, please. I'm so sorry. I'm so sorry. Don't stop loving me, please, Molly, please. I'm so sorry. I'm so sorry.

(*Archie is really sobbing now. Molly is somehow deeply moved. She puts down bread knife, opens her arms, moves to Archie*)

MOLLY: Oh, God . . . come on. Come here.

ARCHIE: I get so mad all the time, Molly. I can't stop myself. I can't stop myself.

MOLLY (*cradling Archie's head in her arms. He weeps*): I know. I know. Shhhhh. Shhhhh. It's okay.

SYLVIE (*hugging Archie as well*): It's okay, Daddy. Don't cry. Don't cry, Daddy. I love you so much, Daddy. Don't cry, Daddy. Please? Please?

(*The entire family, with the single exception of Roddy [the Younger], gathers tightly around Archie, consoling him, comforting him*)

RODDY (THE YOUNGER) (*to audience*): The entire room is now filled with an unexpected tenderness from which I am totally and utterly . . . *excluded.*

(*Roddy [the Younger] moves slowly across kitchen floor to the staircase, past his family, unnoticed. As he climbs the stairs, the lights fade out. End of Act One.*)

ACT TWO

ACT TWO

Scene One

Music in. Lights up on Roddy (the Elder) downstage, carrying chair and steering wheel, which he sets into position downstage center.

RODDY (THE ELDER): As my father never worked weekends, I rarely had a chance to ride in the truck with him . . . except when school was closed for the odd, indigenous Boston holiday like Patriots Day or, say, Cardinal Cushing's birthday. I also used to ride to the mills with him on major Jewish holidays like Rosh Hashona and Yom Kippur. (*Pauses*) Sylvie, never. In her entire life, not once. (*Pauses*) Sylvie and I weren't allowed to go to school on Jewish holidays . . . because we were Jewish. Of course, we didn't ever actually go to synagogue because my father thought the local rabbi, who was a dentist full-time and a rabbi part-time, was only in the rabbinical game to have secret meetings with many, many married Jewish women who were active in the Temple Sisterhood. But, that's another story.

(*Roddy [the Elder] begins to "drive" his truck . . . acts shifting gears and turning steering wheel*)

RODDY (THE ELDER): . . . . Because my father was himself raised as a synagogue-going Jew, he felt that he had to somehow observe the holiday, even though he was in a truck, on a highway, far from makeshift temples and fornicating rabbis. So he said his High Holiday prayers in his Chevy flatbed, on the way to the Felulah Mills in Fitchburg, Massachusetts.

(*Roddy [the Younger] enters carrying another chair, sets it down beside Archie, sits, takes over the narration*)

RODDY (THE YOUNGER): And I got to ride along with him . . . and Willie.

(*Willie enters, carrying a chair which he places sideways next to Roddy's chair. Willie sits with arm on chair's back, as if resting on truck window ledge. Roddy [the Younger] is sandwiched between the two grownups in a truck-cabin designed for two. The truck lurches left . . . and then right. The three men sway, side to side, appropriately. Suddenly, Willie spots something. He leans his head out of truck window, like a large dog. He begins whistling and cat-calling to an unseen female passerby.* NOTE: The actor who has been playing Roddy [the Elder] is now again playing Archie)

WILLIE (*five shrill whistles first; then screaming*): *Hey, hey, hey, heyyyy, Hedy Lamar! Where'd you get those gambinos! Wanna wrap 'em around my coconuts?!* (*Shrill whistles again*)

ARCHIE: Not in front of the boy, Willie!

WILLIE (*leaning out of window. Shrill whistles again; screaming to unseen female passerby again*): Stuck-up, conceited bitch! Stick your nose up in the air any higher and I'll hav'ta climb a tree to dick ya!

ARCHIE: Did'ya hear me say "Not in front of the boy," Willie?

WILLIE (*leaning out, still glaring at unseen passerby*): Oh, look'it that, Arch! I get it! She's *with* somebody, Arch! This is why we're not gettin' the time of day! . . . There you go! This is the reason we're getting *nothin'* off a her, Arch! Jesus, she's *kissin'* the lucky bast'id! (*Calls out to unseen man*) Hey, you lucky bast'id! Bring your mother and father around and I'll *marry* them! OOoooo, Gawd bless us! She's tonguin' him, Arch! (*Calls out to unseen couple*) Parlez-vous Frenchie kiss-kiss! Oui oui oui!

ARCHIE: Not in front of the boy, Willie, will ya?!

WILLIE: Roddy probably knows twice as much as us both put together, Arch, huh?

(*Willie squeezes Roddy [the Younger]'s leg*)

WILLIE: Don'tcha', Rod, huh? (*Tousles Roddy [the Younger]'s hair*) I'll bet they don't call ya "Rod" for nothin', right?

ARCHIE: What are you? Demented?

WILLIE: Let the kid answer for himself. (*Tousles Roddy [the Younger]'s hair again*) I'll bet they don't call ya "Rod" for nothin', huh?

RODDY (THE YOUNGER): I guess not.

ARCHIE (*to Roddy [the Younger]*): What are you saying, you?

WILLIE (*illustrating his point graphically*): I'm just sayin' I'll bet they don't call yo'r boy "Rod" for nothin'.

ARCHIE: I'm talkin' to him. Why do you think we named you Roddy?

RODDY (THE YOUNGER): Because you had an Uncle Rodney who died and you loved him, and you named me for him.

ARCHIE (*to Roddy [the Younger]*): Exactly. (*To Willie*) This is the way it's done in the Jewish faith, Willie.

WILLIE: Hey listen, no problem, Arch. (*Suddenly Willie leans out of window; screams to new unseen female passerby*) *Is that your ass or are you stealing basketballs?*

(*Roddy giggles*)

ARCHIE: Not in front of the boy!

WILLIE: Hey, whoa, slow down, Arch, slow down, slow down, slow down! *Look, look, look, look, look!*

(*Archie acts downshifting gears, slows and stops truck. . . . The three men playact watching unseen female passerby walk across street in front of truck. Their eyes follow her, slowly, from right to left*)

ARCHIE (*laughing*): You're right. She's stealing basketballs.

(*Roddy sees his father laugh; laughs loudly*)

WILLIE: Your boy's laughin', Arch! He gets it! Little Rod gets the joke, Arch!

ARCHIE: What's so funny, you?

RODDY (THE YOUNGER): I think she's stealing *watermelons.*

WILLIE (*roaring with laughter; tousling Roddy [the Younger]'s hair*): Watermelons, Archie! Did you hear your kid? *Watermelons!*

ARCHIE (*unable to hide his pride*): I heard him.

(*Willie looks out of window at unseen passersby; giggles, out of context; tousles Roddy [the Younger]'s hair*)

WILLIE (*philosophically*): I'm gonna tell ya what's really great about getting up at four o'clock in the mornin' and riding a truck the way we do, Little Rod: What's really great about getting up at four o'clock in the mornin' and riding a truck the way we do is you get an opportunity to see many, many first-shift female factory workers in many, many neighborhoods. In Wakefield, Stoneham, Woburn, you get your many laundry-girls and dry-cleaning plant workers . . . clean, starched uniforms. Oh, yummy yummy yum yum! You can just *taste* what's underneath!

ARCHIE: What is *with* you? Are you brain-damaged, or what?

WILLIE: Lynn, Beverly, Salem, Swampscott, Marblehead, Gloucester give you your many female fish-plant workers . . . your female fish-stick packers and your female cutters. This is the other end of the globe from a point of view of clean-hands kinda thing. Your female fish-plant workers are bloody and thinkin' about death all the time. They're also thinkin', "Life's tough, so, why not?" . . . This makes them readily available to the passing stranger, especially if he's a sharp dresser with a good sense of humor and a long stiff tongue such as *moi!* (*Archie begins to rock forward and back, slowly mumbling a Hebrew prayer under his breath. Willie stops talking, looks at Archie*) What's gives, Arch? You feelin' car-sick again?

ARCHIE: I'm praying. It's a Jewish High Holiday!

WILLIE: No problem, Arch.

RODDY (THE YOUNGER) (*looking up at Archie*): Me too?

ARCHIE: Did you convert? Are you an Episcopalian now? (*Roddy [the Younger] clasps his hands together, closes his eyes . . . imitates Archie by rocking back and forth slowly . . . prays. Willie stares at both of them for a few moments silently. Then he looks up at heaven, crosses himself . . . and he too begins to pray. They all pray for a few moments, as Archie continues to "drive" the truck millward*) Red light.

(*Archie acts pulling truck to a stop at imagined red light.*

They all continue to pray for a moment until suddenly, Willie notices an unseen beauty in car stopped next to them at red light. He smiles to heaven gratefully)

WILLIE (*to God*): My prayers have been answered! (*Leans out of window, speaks to unseen beauty*) Hullo, Baby-Dollface! Whose little girl are you? Wanna suck a lollipop?

(*Archie and Roddy [the Younger] are astonished. Both stop praying. Both roll their eyes to heaven.*

Lights switch to black. After two count, lights restore. Willie is gone, his chair is empty)

RODDY (THE YOUNGER): From time to time, Willie would go off on what my father would call "a sex fiend's errands," and my father and I would be left alone to talk about life together. We were not what you might call *naturally comfortable* with each other.

ARCHIE: So, well, uh, Rod . . . how's school?

RODDY (THE YOUNGER): School's good, Dad.

ARCHIE: School's good, huh?

RODDY (THE YOUNGER): Oh, yuh, school's good.

ARCHIE: That's good.

(*There is a substantial pause*)

ARCHIE: How's your sister?

RODDY (THE YOUNGER): Sylvie?

ARCHIE: Well, Sylvie's your sister, yes?

RODDY (THE YOUNGER): Well, you see her as much as I do.

ARCHIE: Not as much. You see her after I go off to work and, you know, before I come home. And if I go to bed early, you sometimes stay up talking to her and all.

(*There is a small pause*)

RODDY (THE YOUNGER): I think she's fine.

ARCHIE: You think so?

RODDY (THE YOUNGER): I do. I mean she's never said she's *not* fine . . . not to me privately.

ARCHIE: I'm glad to hear this.

RODDY (THE YOUNGER) (*to audience*): After a minute or so of silence, while he tried to find a subtle way to ask me what he *really* wanted to ask me, he'd, well, *give up* and just *ask* me . . . straight out.

ARCHIE: Does your sister ever talk to you about her doing weird things with boys?

RODDY (THE YOUNGER): Oh God, never! I don't think she even *knows* any boys . . . except, ya know, you, me and Grandpa. Uncle Arnold.

ARCHIE: If she ever talks to you about doing weird things with boys, you'll say something to me, right?

RODDY (THE YOUNGER) (*to Archie quietly*): Sure, I will.

ARCHIE: It's for her own good. You know this, yes?

RODDY (THE YOUNGER): Sure.

ARCHIE: You promise me on this?

RODDY (THE YOUNGER): Sure. I promise. (*Glances to heaven privately, grimaces*)

ARCHIE: Your mother never says anything oddball to you, does she?

RODDY (THE YOUNGER): Mama? Uh-uh.

ARCHIE: Never?

RODDY (THE YOUNGER): Mama? Never. (*Pauses*) Grandma neither. If either of them ever do, though, I'll tell you right away.

ARCHIE: Good.

RODDY (THE YOUNGER) (*to audience*): We played endless variations on this particular theme of Sylvie, Mama and/or Grandma's saying and/or doing weird and/or oddball things to and/or with men. And each time, when the interrogation was done, my father and I would ride through a thousand embarrassed pauses as pregnant as the harlot Sylvie of my father's wildest dreams. We shared these silences as though the passing landscape were somehow, suddenly, *intriguing*, as though we weren't suffering the pain of such shared *awkwardness*. (*Archie and Roddy [the Younger] now stare straight ahead sadly, each avoiding visual or spiritual contact with the other. For this brief moment, each is undeniably alone, each is undeniably in pain. Over the scene, we have been hearing a small musical refrain, probably Chopin. When music ends, Roddy [the Younger] talks to audience directly*) It happened on an October morning. School was cancelled for a teachers' convention and Willie was off Godknowswhere doing Godknowswhat to Godknowswhom. My father and I had done the morning mill-run to Fitchburg without saying a single word. On the trip back home, on a back road somewhere near Leominister, Massachusetts, my father broke the silence.

(*Archie looks at Roddy [the Younger]. The boy returns the look. They share a silent stare for a moment. Then Archie speaks*)

ARCHIE: Rod?

RODDY (THE YOUNGER): Yes, sir?

ARCHIE: You like to play baseball, don't you?

RODDY (THE YOUNGER): I do, yuh.

ARCHIE: Are you any good?

RODDY (THE YOUNGER): I could be better, I guess.

ARCHIE: Can you hit?

RODDY (THE YOUNGER): I can hit okay. I'm a great fielder . . . not ground balls so much as fly balls. I can catch 'em.

ARCHIE: That's great. (*Pauses*) It's a pain in the neck I don't get much of a chance to play ball with you.

RODDY (THE YOUNGER): That's okay. Mama plays with me a lot. She can't really hit 'em hard, but it's still practice.

ARCHIE: We don't do much together, I mean.

RODDY (THE YOUNGER): It's okay. (*Brightly*) We get to ride in the truck together.

ARCHIE: You like doin' this?

RODDY (THE YOUNGER): Are you kidding me? I love this!

ARCHIE (*happily*): Me, too. (*Both stare straight ahead. Both are smiling*) How's your Red Feather speech coming?

RODDY (THE YOUNGER): Oh, well, it's okay.

ARCHIE: It's getting close, huh?

RODDY (THE YOUNGER): Four weeks, three days . . . (*Looks at Archie's wristwatch*) . . . sixteen hours. (*Pauses*) If I win my school, I get to go on to the subregionals, and maybe, you know, the New England Finals and all.

ARCHIE (*whistling appreciatively*): Big stuff, huh?

RODDY (THE YOUNGER): Oh yuh. The national winner gets a $2,000 college scholarship. I could pay my own way kind of thing.

ARCHIE: Scared?

RODDY (THE YOUNGER): Me? About the contest? Not too much. I just wish it was, you know, better.

ARCHIE: What was better?

RODDY (THE YOUNGER): My speech.

ARCHIE: Wanna try it on me?

RODDY (THE YOUNGER): You kidding?

ARCHIE: Naw. What the heck . . . it's just us riding together . . . two guys . . . father and son kinda thing. We won't hit home plate for at least an hour. How long is it?

RODDY (THE YOUNGER): My speech? Three minutes.

ARCHIE: That's all?

RODDY (THE YOUNGER): Oh yuh. There's a time limit.

ARCHIE: That's all the whole speech is?

RODDY (THE YOUNGER): Well, yuh . . . yes. We also get an extemporaneous part to do.

ARCHIE: Oh yuh, right.

RODDY (THE YOUNGER) (*sensing Archie's confusion, explaining gently*): That means they give you a subject right then and there, and you have to make up a speech on that subject with no preparation . . .

ARCHIE: Just sort of make it up on the spot kind of thing?

RODDY (THE YOUNGER): Exactly.

ARCHIE: You're probably good at that.

RODDY (THE YOUNGER): Oh yuh. I'm better at that part than the prepared part . . . you know . . . "We have nothing to fear but fear itself" kind of thing.

ARCHIE: What's this?

RODDY (THE YOUNGER): That's my prepared part. I could do some of it for you. I wouldn't have to do the whole three minutes. I could just do the start of it.

ARCHIE: No, no, no. Do the whole thing.

RODDY (THE YOUNGER): Really?

ARCHIE: Sure. Why not? I mean, as long as we're doing things together, we might as well do *whole* things together, right?

RODDY (THE YOUNGER): Well, yuh, *sure!* The thing is, I'm not really finished.

ARCHIE: Do whatever you've got.

RODDY (THE YOUNGER): Well, okay . . . (*Clears his throat*) Are you sure you wanna hear this, Daddy? You don't have to! . . . I mean, I've got plenty of other people who don't mind . . .

ARCHIE: Come on! Let me hear it!

RODDY (THE YOUNGER): Well . . . okay . . . sure. (*Clears his throat*) "We have nothing to fear but fear itself." That famous quotation was spoken by President Franklin Delano Roosevelt . . .

ARCHIE: Roosevelt said this?

RODDY (THE YOUNGER): He did, yuh.

ARCHIE: Roosevelt was a Jew-hating bastard!

RODDY (THE YOUNGER): I know. I talk about this in my speech.

ARCHIE: You don't say "bastard" in front of your teacher, do you?

RODDY (THE YOUNGER): No, no. I use a different word.

ARCHIE: Let me hear.

RODDY (THE YOUNGER): "We have nothing to fear but fear itself." That famous quotation was spoken by President Franklin Delano Roosevelt as he and many, many other Jew-hating maniacs plunged this great Nation into War! . . .

ARCHIE: "Maniacs" . . . good . . . I like "maniacs."

RODDY (THE YOUNGER): I tried it different ways, but I liked "maniacs" best of all. Maybe I should wait till I get it finished more.

ARCHIE: No, no, no. I like hearing your speech. I like doing this . . . just us kinda thing.

RODDY (THE YOUNGER) (*doing the first part again rapidly, skipping over the lines to get to the yet-unspoken lines*): "We have nothing to fear but fear itself." That famous quotation was spoken by President Franklin Delano Roosevelt as he and many, many other Jew-hating maniacs plunged this great Nation into War! . . . (*Having recapitulated the start of the speech, Roddy now slows his delivery down to a proper pace)* What did President Roosevelt mean, exactly, when he uttered that famous quote? Did he mean that the things that scare us most aren't real? That they're imagined things . . . like ghosts and boogey-men; which we, after all, know aren't real? . . .

ARCHIE: Ghosts may be real.

RODDY (THE YOUNGER): You think so?

ARCHIE: I dunno. I have this really weird kinda sense of my Uncle Herman all the time. . . . He was a Rabinowitz, on my mother's side. Uncle Herman Rabinowitz was kind of, you know, crazy. He was actually very crazy. He used to whistle in public . . . patriotic marches . . . from Poland. I think they were from Poland. He was arrested for exposing himself. You know what that means?

RODDY (THE YOUNGER): Not exactly . . . kind of. Like showing your private parts to people kind of thing?

ARCHIE: Sort of . . . it means more like showing your private parts to people who don't really want to *see* your private parts kind of thing.

RODDY (THE YOUNGER): Oh, sure, right . . . I get you.

ARCHIE: Uncle Herman Rabinowitz did this a lot.

RODDY (THE YOUNGER): Gosh.

ARCHIE: He was arrested. Uncle Herman said he was peeing, but the lady who turned him in said he was doing more than that. (*Pauses*) Don't ever tell your grandmother I told you any of this stuff, okay?

RODDY (THE YOUNGER): I won't! . . .

ARCHIE: You've gotta promise!

RODDY (THE YOUNGER): I promise!

ARCHIE: Good.

RODDY (THE YOUNGER): Would you mind if I waited to show you the rest of my speech til I've done a little more work on it?

ARCHIE: Hey, you're the boss! It's *your* speech.

RODDY (THE YOUNGER): Really?

ARCHIE: Sure!

(*There is a moment's pause during which both men are smiling. Then, Roddy pops The Big Question*)

RODDY (THE YOUNGER): When do you think you could teach me to steer?

ARCHIE: You're not s'posed ta touch a wheel til you're sixteen! . . . You're not allowed! This is Massachusetts! I could go to jail for letting you steer! Sixteen's the law! . . .

RODDY (THE YOUNGER): You told me Grandpa taught you to steer when you were my age.

ARCHIE: That was different! We had no money! . . . (*Archie acts pulling truck over to side of road, stops*) Come on, over here.

(*Roddy [the Younger] squeezes into Archie's "embrace," as Roddy clutches steering wheel and Archie guides him. Roddy pretends to steer truck. Both men are, for the moment, very, very happy*)

RODDY (*to audience*): We rode together that way, me on his lap steering . . . he with his arms around me, guiding me, sharing an against-the-law risk with me for at least four minutes.

ARCHIE: That's enough.

(*Archie stops the truck; Roddy [the Younger] relinquishes the steering wheel, slides away from Archie; looks out to audience directly*)

RODDY (THE YOUNGER): In my entire childhood, I only remember my father hugging me that one time.

(*The lights crossfade to . . .*)

ACT TWO

Scene Two

Haddie shuffles on, calls out to Roddy (the Younger).

HADDIE: Okay, Roddy, I'm ready to listen to your speech now.

(*Haddie moves to stove, makes cup of tea for herself as Roddy [the Younger] moves to her, practicing his speech*)

RODDY (THE YOUNGER): Okay, Grandma . . . here goes. . . . What President Roosevelt was teaching us was to get over our fears before they cripple us . . . the way polio crippled *him*—Roosevelt—who was a cripple. So, when Roosevelt says, "We have nothing to fear but fear itself," he's telling us to find the courage to confront the thing itself instead of our fear of the thing itself before we ourselves become crippled like Roosevelt who, of course, got crippled by polio, not fear. (*Pauses, confused; disgusted by still another lamentable failure. He mouthes an appropriate word, behind his grandmother's back*) [Shit!]

HADDIE: Maybe you'd better not type it up just yet.

(*Haddie takes tea bag from teacup, tosses tea bag into waste-basket, crosses upstage to kitchen table; sits, waits for Roddy to join her.*

The lights crossfade with Roddy [the Younger], who moves into spotlight downstage right; speaks to audience directly)

RODDY (THE YOUNGER): Just before my Grandma Haddie died, she told me the most amazing thing about my family, Grandpa Jacob included.

(*Lights crossfade from Roddy back to Haddie. Roddy crosses to table, sits next to Haddie*)

HADDIE: The men in our family are crazy people, all of them! They think every woman is loose! My own father, may his soul rest in peace, used to make my mother wear an over-coat all through the summer, so no man could see that she had big breasts. In the meantime, my father's own uncle Duddy, on the Zuckerman side, may his soul never rest a minute, used to touch me in private places when I was a very little girl. His wife said he used to light fires in front of pictures of naked ladies. Your own grandfather is no picnic himself. In all the years we've been married, which is forty-seven, he has never once let me shop alone. He was not only convinced the butcher was after me, he was also convinced that I was after the butcher! Once he kicked a hole in the dining room wall because I let the butcher sell me an extra-lean rib roast. (*Shrugs*) Go figure! . . . (*Continues*) I used to tell him, "You're just like your father!" and this would always drive your grandfather crazy because he really hated his father, your great-grand-father, who used to yell things at women on the street that you should never know about! God forbid! . . . I'm going to tell you something, Roddy. No matter how crazy your grandfather got when I told him he was just like his father, I'm telling you he was *just* like his father! Maybe worse. Your own father (my son) I don't have to tell you much about because you're *living* in the story, yourself, yes? But, I have to tell you one story . . . from the zoo in Stoneham, when he was little. Your grandfather and I took him there on a very sunny Sunday morning. There was a crowd in front of the lion's cage and we were way at the back. . . . So, Arthur, your father, squeezed in through the people, up to the front, all by himself. When he got there—to the front—for some reason, the lion roared. It was really quite a roar. Long, loud, really enormous. Everybody—all of us, kids and grownups—got scared. And then, we all laughed. But, I knew your father would have gotten very scared, so I pushed my way up front. When I got to him, he was off to one side, roaring like a lion. There were tears all over his face and his sailor shirt but, he was roaring really loud, just like the lion. The sound coming out of him was enormous. I let him roar for a while, until he got himself calmed down. (*Pauses*) Sometimes people do this, Roddy. . . . Sometimes people have to imitate the things that scare them the most. (*Haddie pauses; moves to Roddy; speaks to him confidentially*) I'm only telling you any of this because, between us, I don't like these shooting pains in my head I'm getting, and somebody's got to talk straight to you, before you yourself start, you know, roaring.

RODDY (THE YOUNGER): I'm never going to do any roaring, Grandma.

HADDIE: Fine. I'm glad to hear this, but maybe you should try to remember my story, just in case you ever hear yourself roar a *little.*

RODDY (THE YOUNGER): I will.

HADDIE: Good.

RODDY (THE YOUNGER): You have pains in your head, Grandma?

HADDIE: This is between us. Promise me.

RODDY (THE YOUNGER): I promise you. (*Pauses*) I'm sure you're going to be fine, Grandma!

HADDIE: Maybe I don't *want* to be fine? Maybe enough is enough. (*Pauses; smiles*) Let me say what I'm trying to say to you, simply and clearly, Rodney. . . . All of the men in this family are crazy people. Wait. You'll see.

(*Haddie's light fades out.*)

ACT TWO

Scene Three

Roddy (the Younger) moves into spotlight, downstage right; speaks to audience, directly.

RODDY (THE YOUNGER): We always thought Grandpa would die before Grandma. I guess we *hoped* he would. So when Grandma died, like she did, before Grandpa, we didn't know what we were going to do with him.

(*Lights crossfade with Roddy [the Younger] as he moves to Jacob. Offstage, we hear the sound of Kaddish, the Hebrew prayer for the dead*)

RODDY (THE YOUNGER): We should go back into the front room now, Grandpa. They're saying Kaddish again.

JACOB: They've got their ten men. They've got *twenty* men! (*Leans in, discreetly*) Your grandmother had a lot of men-friends, Roddy.

RODDY (THE YOUNGER): You think so?

JACOB: I *know* so. (*Looks at Roddy smugly*) That's all I'm going to say on this subject.

RODDY (THE YOUNGER) (*to audience*): Grandpa Jacob's Parkinsonian stutter cleared up the minute Grandma Haddie was in her grave.

JACOB: It was hell being married forty-seven years to a beauty like your grandmother, Roddy. If I can give you one piece of advice, straight from my heart, when you're ready to get married, find the ugliest woman you can find . . . somebody so horrible other men will avert their eyes when she passes. This woman, if she has any brains at all, will know how unappealing she is to the male multitude, and she will love you for marrying her . . . and she will serve you, without any of the pain I had with a beauty like your grandmother. This is advice from my heart, Roddy. I gave this advice to your father and he didn't take it, and now look at him!

(*Jacob motions to window. Archie is outside, peering into the house suspiciously. After a moment, Archie disappears from the window*)

RODDY (THE YOUNGER): Do you think all of the men in our family are crazy, Grandpa?

JACOB: Did your grandmother suggest this to you?

RODDY (THE YOUNGER): She did, yes.

JACOB: Your grandmother knew a lot about people, Rodney . . . especially men!

(*We hear the sound of male voices singing Kaddish. Molly enters. She is in mourning, wears a black dress; calls out to Jacob*)

MOLLY: Get in here, Pa! They're saying Kaddish!

JACOB (*screaming suddenly*): For *her*, not for *me!* I'm not dead!

MOLLY: Who said you were dead? (*To Roddy [the Younger]*) Did I say such a thing?

RODDY (THE YOUNGER): It's the prayer for Grandma, Grandpa. Come on, I'll go inside with you.

JACOB: No! You're just a young boy! I don't want you in there! Young boys shouldn't have to see such things. (*Motions to Molly*) She'll take me in.

MOLLY: Come on, Pa. Grab ahold.

(*Molly leans in, places Jacob's hands on her shoulders, starts to lift him from his chair. Jacob begins to cry; yells at Molly directly*)

JACOB: How could she leave me alone by myself with people like *you?* How *could* she? *How?*

(*Again we hear male voices singing Kaddish under the scene, as Jacob continues to sob openly now, calling Haddie's name in Yiddish*)

JACOB: Haddelah . . . mein Haddelah . . . Haddelah . . . liebling . . .

MOLLY (*quietly*): Come on, Pa . . . I'll take you in.

(*Molly leads Jacob into room. He walks backwards, she walks forward . . . as if in a waltz*)

RODDY (THE YOUNGER) (*to audience*): Grandpa Jacob died that night. We all heard it . . . his scream. It would have been too corny, even for Grandpa Jacob's favorite radio show, "Portia Faces Life."

JACOB (*screaming, from off in the darkness*): *I don't want to live without her! Arrrrhhhh!*

RODDY (THE YOUNGER): We knew he would be dead when we went in there.

(*Lights up in kitchen suddenly, as Roddy [the Younger], Sylvie and Molly run to door of back bedroom; stop before entering*)

MOLLY: *Pa?*

RODDY (THE YOUNGER): *Grandpa!*

SYLVIE: *Grandpa!*

ARCHIE (*off*): *Paaa?*

(*Archie runs downstairs, crosses kitchen to Jacob's bedroom, runs inside. Beat. He screams*)

ARCHIE (*off*): *Paaaaaaaaaaaa!*

(*Music in: Again we hear male voices singing Kaddish, offstage.*

Roddy [the Younger], Sylvie, Archie and Molly stand framed in doorway to Jacob's bedroom. They bow their heads and weep as music concludes. Lights crossfade to . . .)

ACT TWO

Scene Four

Spotlight downstage center on Roddy (the Younger), who faces audience. Music in: Chopin étude, lightly played on piano.

RODDY (THE YOUNGER): The night after Grandpa Jacob died, I was laying awake thinking about things, and it crossed my mind that when Roosevelt said, "We have nothing to fear but fear itself," he could have been completely full of shit! We have *plenty* to fear! . . . We have old age to fear. We have loneliness and disease to fear. We have some very crazy people around us all the time to fear! We also have things like Red Feather Oratory Contests to fear! And we also have The Worst to fear. (*Pauses*) The Worst happened to me and my family on the morning of the Red Feather Regionals. If I live to be sixty, I will always wonder if either Grandpa Jacob or Grandma Haddie had lived just a little longer and had been alive that day . . . if either of them had been, you know, home in the house with Mama, whether it would've changed anything . . . or whether all bad things are *meant to happen* and they just do; they just *happen*, no matter what. (*Lights widen, lighting kitchen and Molly at piano, playing Chopin. She is wearing her bathrobe and bedroom slippers. A man is peering through the upstage right window into the house from outside.* NOTE: audience should assume the man is Archie. *The man disappears from window, as suddenly as he had appeared. Roddy [the Younger] continues speaking to the audience directly*) He must have come into the house around ten-thirty in the morning. Sylvie and I were both in school What I remember most of all about the day was that I learned about Congressional Franking Privileges. Sylvie says she has no memory of the day whatsoever.

Daddy was supposed to be with Willie in Fitchburg, unloading the truck. But, Willie had called in sick with the Virus-X. (*The man suddenly reappears at other window; peers in at Molly. We now see that it is Willie in window, not Archie. Molly continues to play, oblivious to Willie in window. Willie disappears from window suddenly, then reappears at door. He knocks on door three times. Molly, intent on her piano-playing, doesn't hear him*) There are moments that redefine an afternoon, and there are moments that redefine a life. This was, alas, a moment to redefine my entire family.

(*Roddy [the Younger] exits up staircase as Willie enters house, stops and watches Molly play.*

Molly senses Willie's presence in room and, certain it is Archie who has entered, she whirls around, away from piano)

MOLLY: I was only seeing if the piano was out of tune! . . . (*Sees it's Willie, not Archie*) Willie.

WILLIE: I didn't know you played piano. You play wickid good, don'tcha?

MOLLY (*re-belting her robe tightly*): You shouldn't be in the house, Willie.

WILLIE: I was feelin' a lot better after my nap, so I hopped on over here to see if I could catch Arch before his second mill-run.

MOLLY: Archie's not here. He left over an hour ago.

WILLIE (*appreciating her body*): Archie never talks about you playing the piano, Moll. Never mentions it ever. You play classical, too. Sophisticated. (*Looks around room; smiles*) It's nice bein' in the house with you, just us, like this. It's a shame about Archie's folks and all. Still and all, they lived life, didn't they? I mean, that's what life's for, ain't it . . .

livin'. Ain't it, Moll? (*Looks Molly over*) You're lookin' good, Molly. I was just sayin' this very thing ta Arch, not all that long ago: Molly's lookin' wickid good. (*Laughs; looks Molly over again*) You really are lookin' wickid good, Moll. You're puttin' on weight in all the right places. Not that you're lookin' heavy. I ain't sayin' that. You're lookin', I dunno, what's the word? . . . Comfortable. Some women are built for speed, but you're very definitely built for comfort.

MOLLY: You shouldn't be in the house, Willie. You're not allowed. You know this.

WILLIE: *Allowed?* I'm not *allowed?* (*He laughs*) That's a funny thing you just said, Moll. (*Moves to door of back bedroom; peeks inside*) This is where they slept, huh? The old ones. (*Smiles at Molly*) Must be lonely in the house for you now, huh, Moll? . . . Kids at school . . . Arch off somewhere in the truck as he is. . . . Just a good-lookin' girl like you alone in a big house like this. (*Moves to staircase; looks upstairs*) I never be'n upstairs. Weird, huh? All these years workin' for Arch and all, and I never be'n upstairs in his house. I mean, he's be'n upstairs in *my* house plenty, right?

MOLLY: You can't be in the house, Willie. You're going to have to leave now.

WILLIE: I don't think so.

MOLLY: Willie, please! I must insist you leave the house.

WILLIE (*staring at Molly; smiling*): Uh-uh.

MOLLY: Willie, please? I'm asking you nicely.

(*She opens door for Willie to leave*)

Steve Ryan *(right)* as Archie with Jonathan Marc Sherman as Roddy (the Younger) in the 1994 WPA Theater production of "Unexpected Tenderness." *Photo by Carol Rosegg.*

Paula Plum *(right)* as Molly with Be
Webster as Roddy (the Younger) i
the 1994 Gloucester Stage Compa
production of "Unexpected
Tenderness." *Photo by Tsar Fedorsky*

(From left to right) Sol Frieder as Jacob, Scottie Bloch as Haddie, Karen Goberman as Sylvie, Steve Ryan as Archie and Caitlin Clarke as Molly in the 1994 WPA Theater production of "Unexpected Tenderness." *Photo by Carol Rosegg.*

Judy Holmes *(center)* as Beverley with David Jones *(left)* as Archie and Marina Re *(right)* as Cecily in the 1993 Gloucester Stage Company Production of "Fighting Over Beverley." *Photo by Tsar Fedorsky.*

Priscilla Shanks *(right)* as Cecily with Elizabeth ilson in the 1994 tamford Theatre Vorks production f "Fighting Over everley." *Photo by Jayson Byrd*

Elizabeth Wilson *(center)* with John Braden *(left)* as Zelly and George Taylo *(right)* as Archie in the 1994 Stamford Theatre Works production of "Fighti Over Beverley." *Photo by Jayson Byrd.*

WILLIE: Oh, well, if you put it that way . . . (*Willie starts to door, as if he's leaving . . . but then he slams door closed, confronts Molly*) Not a chance. (*Sees Molly looking about furtively*) How come you're talking like somebody else is listening? Nobody's listening! It's just us.

(*Willie caresses Molly's cheek, pushing her hair out of her eyes. Molly is stunned. She cannot possibly misinterpret Willie's intentions. She steps backwards from him stiffly*)

MOLLY: Willie, get out of this house!

WILLIE (*moving toward her again*): You like me, don't you, Moll?

MOLLY: If you don't leave, *I'll* leave.

(*Molly starts to door. Willie blocks her path. At same moment,* Archie appears in window, peering inside house; *sees Willie, pulls back; disappears from window*)

MOLLY: Willie, get out of my way! . . . I want to go outside.

WILLIE: In your bathrobe? You wanna go outside in your bathrobe, Molly?

(*Willie starts to move slowly toward Molly, laughing. Molly backs up, terrified*)

MOLLY: Willie!

WILLIE: I seen you lookin' at me, for years and years now, four mornin's a week, never changin' outta your bathrobe til after I'm gone and all, right? . . . Flashing this and that at me . . . smilin' at me, makin' my lunches and all . . . askin' all the time if my coughs and colds are gettin' better kinda thing! I seen and felt all this *attraction* coming from you, Moll.

(*Molly looks inside kitchen drawer for bread knife. It's not there. Willie steps forward, tries to embrace Molly. She slaps his face. It is a stunning blow. Willie staggers backward, shakes his head clear; laughs*)

WILLIE: I knew you'd fight me!

(*Willie steps in, grabs Molly firmly, tries to kiss her. She wriggles and screams, trying to get loose from him. Suddenly the door opens; Archie enters the kitchen. He is ashen*)

WILLIE: Jesus, Arch! You look wickid pissed! . . . Take it easy, Arch, huh? I can explain myself here! . . . She invited me in, Arch. I woulda gladly waited outside, like you said, but she . . . (*Archie moves past Willie wordlessly; goes directly to Molly; slaps her. She screams; falls backwards against table. Archie slaps her again. Willie stares at Archie, amazed*) Jesus, Arch! What are you doin'? What are you hittin' her for?

(*Archie never looks at Willie. Instead, he slaps Molly again*)

ARCHIE: Your boyfriend's askin' what I'm doing. You hear him? (*Molly doesn't reply*) You're not answering me?

(*No reply. Archie slaps Molly again*)

WILLIE (*horrified*): Jesus! Nothin' happened between us, Arch! Honest ta God! You gotta calm yourself down, Arch, before you do damage!

ARCHIE: Whoaaa! You hear this? (*No reply. Archie slaps Molly again*) Your boyfriend's protecting you. Do you not hear him? (*Archie raises his hand to hit Molly again. Willie reaches in to stop him; barely touches Archie who recoils from his touch violently*) No touches, you! *No touches!* (*Archie slaps Molly again*) Every time your boyfriend protects you, you're getting hit! You get me! *You get me?*

WILLIE: Jesus, Arch! . . . Jesus!

(*Willie turns, runs out of door*)

ARCHIE (*in a murderous rage; standing ready to hit Molly again*): I seen this coming, lady, believe-you-me! You couldn't even wait til my mother and father were cold in the grave, could you? Could you? *Could you?*

(*Archie raises his hand; moves to hit Molly. . . . The lights black out.*)

ACT TWO

Scene Five

In the darkness we hear microphone feedback and then announcer's voice over public address system, heavy Boston accent.

ANNOUNCER'S VOICE: Ladies and gentlemen, our next competitor in the Red Feather Oratory Contest New England Finals is our youngest competitor. He is a 15-year-old high school student from Wakefield, Massachusetts. Welcome, please, Rodney Stern!

(*We hear applause. Spotlight fades up on Roddy [the Younger] upstage, near piano. He delivers his Red Feather Oratory Contest speech . . . with poise, confidence . . . and appropriate hand gestures*)

RODDY (THE YOUNGER): Fellow Red Feather Oratory Contest competitors, judges, ladies and gentlemen . . . "We have nothing to fear but fear itself." When President Franklin Delano Roosevelt spoke those words, he was trying to trick the citizens of the United States of America into finally going to war against Hitler. FDR knew America should have gotten into the war, years and years before, but Roosevelt was waiting as long as he could, hoping that Hitler would kill all the Jews first, because Franklin Delano Roosevelt, like Adolph Hitler, hated the Jews. Finally, after the Japanese bombed Pearl Harbor and killed some non-Jewish Americans, Roosevelt knew he couldn't wait any longer. He declared war on Japan . . . and on Japan's teammate: Hitler. (*Pauses*) The only thing that's kept a lot of people from saying all this stuff about Roosevelt out loud is fear. I myself felt a lot of fear thinking about saying this out loud in my Red Feather Oratory Contest speech, but it's the truth and nobody should ever be frightened to speak the truth, should they? (*Roddy [the Younger] pauses, allowing his question to hang on the air. The lights fade up in the kitchen. Molly enters, carrying two suitcases which she sets down on floor near back door. She is badly bruised; battered. She busies herself, preparing to close up the house. She checks to see that the gas is off, water faucets are tightly shut, windows are closed and locked, etc.*) To be heroic, you first have to be unlucky enough to find yourself in a terrible situation . . . and then, you have to be lucky enough to find your dignity . . . and that will lead you to do what you have to do.

(*We hear a car horn offstage*)

RODDY (THE YOUNGER) (*calling out to his mother*): The taxi's here!

(*Molly opens back door; calls outside to unseen taxi driver*)

MOLLY: We'll be right out! . . . (*She moves to base of staircase; calls upstairs*) The taxi's here! Are you ready?

SYLVIE (*calling down from upstairs*): I'm ready! . . .

RODDY (THE YOUNGER) (*to audience*): Sylvie went downstairs first. I hung back in my room and hid a copy of my Red Feather Oratory Contest Speech under a loose floorboard in my closet. I started down the stairs, but then I ran back to my room and tossed my signed Williams and Pesky rookie cards under the floorboard with my speech! . . . I don't know why I did that. It's one of my life's few major regrets.

(*Sylvie enters from upstairs. She wears a winter overcoat. She carries suitcase too. She, too, has been crying*)

SYLVIE: I'm ready.

MOLLY: We have to do this.

SYLVIE: I said I'm ready.

MOLLY: It's only a house. It's not a life.

SYLVIE: Fine.

MOLLY: Are you mad at me, Sylvie?

SYLVIE: No. I dunno. Maybe. Maybe I'm just sad.

MOLLY: It's just a house. It's not enough reason to stay.

SYLVIE: Were you and daddy ever happy?

MOLLY: I can't remember.

SYLVIE: You were *never* happy?

MOLLY: I can't remember.

SYLVIE: Why did you have children?

MOLLY: We thought it would make us happy.

SYLVIE: Are you sorry you had us?

MOLLY: What are you saying, you? You and Roddy are the best things that ever happened in my life!

SYLVIE (*sobbing*): Roddy, maybe. But aren't you a little sorry you had *me?*

MOLLY (*moaning*): Oh God, nooo, Sylvie! Don't ever think like that! I love you. I'm so glad that you're my daughter. (*Molly hugs Sylvie, both weeping*) Us girls have got to stick together. (*Taxi horn honks again off. Molly looks up*) Where is he? . . . *Rodney!*

(*Roddy [the Younger] enters down staircase, carrying jacket and suitcase, ready to leave*)

RODDY (THE YOUNGER): Here I am.

MOLLY: Are you ready?

RODDY (THE YOUNGER): I'm ready.

MOLLY: Did you clean your room?

RODDY (THE YOUNGER): I cleaned my room.

MOLLY: You made your bed?

RODDY (THE YOUNGER): I made my bed.

MOLLY (*to Sylvie*): You made *your* bed?

SYLVIE: I made my bed.

MOLLY: Listen to me, children . . . I don't know much, but I know *some*thing. Here's the thing: you can never be what you just were two seconds ago. Things have got to keep changing. This is life. And me, I say, "Thank God for this!"

(Molly and Sylvie exit the house. Roddy pauses at door, sets down his suitcase, turns, speaks to audience. Lights dim in kitchen to spotlight on Roddy)

RODDY (THE YOUNGER): I went to visit my father a couple of days later. He was staying at his cousin's house in Woburn.

(A spotlight fades up on Roddy [the Elder], now playing Archie, *alone downstage, sitting on chair, looking out of unseen window. Roddy [the Younger] goes to him)*

RODDY (THE YOUNGER): Hi, Daddy.

ARCHIE: You're alone?

RODDY (THE YOUNGER): Yes, sir.

ARCHIE: You know where your mother is?

RODDY (THE YOUNGER) (*after a pause*): Yes, sir. I do.

ARCHIE: You're not going to tell me?

RODDY (THE YOUNGER): No, sir.

ARCHIE: You scared of me, Roddy?

RODDY (THE YOUNGER): Yes, sir. A little.

ARCHIE: Don't be. I used ta be scared of my father, too. You saw what my father was like when he got old, yes? In the end, there's nothing to be scared of, believe me.

RODDY (THE YOUNGER): I'm going to stay on living with Mama.

ARCHIE: You're what?

RODDY (THE YOUNGER): I'm, uh, staying on living in with Mama.

ARCHIE: Why?

RODDY (THE YOUNGER): Because I want to.

ARCHIE: Why?

RODDY (THE YOUNGER): Because it's what I want to do.

ARCHIE: Did she poison you against me?

RODDY (THE YOUNGER): No, sir. She didn't say anything either way. I decided this myself.

ARCHIE: It's probably better. If you stick with me, the way I stuck with my father, you'll end up . . .

(*Archie stops, midsentence; sobs. Roddy speaks to audience*)

RODDY (THE YOUNGER): My father never finished his thought. He never told me how exactly I might have ended up, if he hadn't done what he was about to do . . . if he hadn't reached out and cured me of the family disease, once and for all. (*Beat*) I'll never know if my father planned it or whether it was an accidental gift, but in one split second of unexpected tenderness, my father changed my life and the lives of generations to follow. . . . He set us free.

(*Suddenly Archie moans in deep despair*)

ARCHIE: Somebody's got to stop me, Roddy! I'm a crazy person! I can't help myself!

(*Archie continues to sob. Roddy watches his father awhile sadly. Then the boy moves to his father; touches Archie's shoulder. Without warning, Archie backhands his son violently. The sound of the slap is amplified in the auditorium. It echoes, reverberates. Roddy flies backwards; stunned; hurt. Archie sobs again. There is a substantial pause in which the boy will realize that he is free*)

RODDY (THE YOUNGER): Thank you, sir. I . . . I'm going.

(*Roddy returns to staircase; faces audience, completes his contest speech. His voice is amplified*)

RODDY (THE YOUNGER): I want to close by telling you the story of a friend of mine who had to conquer a lot of fear. My friend lived in a little town with his mother and his father and his sister. He wasn't very happy, but he wasn't too *un*happy either. Most of the men in my friend's family were a little crazy. They didn't trust women very much. They always thought women were doing bad things. One day my friend's father hit my friend's mother . . . really beat her up. My friend's mother and father got divorced and my friend had to go to court and decide whether he wanted to live with his mother and his sister, which meant he'd have to move away from his little town, or stay and live with his father. My friend was frightened to leave his town and his school and his friends. . . . He really wanted everything to just stay the way it always was, but that wasn't possible. So my friend thought about everything for a long, long time and finally he thought about what Roosevelt said, "We have nothing to fear but fear itself," and my friend thought that Roosevelt was really right after all: Fear itself was probably the thing we have to be frightened of the most! . . . Even though Roosevelt wasn't the great man everybody thought he was, he had figured something out about life and people could, regardless of his faults, learn a lot from him. My friend found his courage. He chose to live with his mother and move away. I'm telling you this story because I, too, have learned a lot from Franklin Delano Roosevelt, and I also learned a lot from working on this speech. I learned how to think about things . . . I learned how to stand up in front of people . . . and speak my thoughts. For this opportunity, I want to thank the Red Feather Oratory Contest organizers, and I want to thank you: the audience. Thank you.

(*Lights crossfade to Roddy [the Elder], standing downstage. He speaks directly to audience*)

RODDY (THE ELDER): My mother found her dignity and she was *heroic!* She and my sister and I moved in with my mother's cousins. After a couple of months, we moved into our own apartment. It wasn't a beautiful place, but it was partly furnished . . . with a piano. (*Light fades up on Molly at piano, playing Chopin nocturne*) My mother learned to play Chopin and Bach and Brahms. We woke every morning to her playing, and fell asleep every night, same way. Our house was full of music. My mother never married again. She said, "One marriage was enough." Sylvie never married either. She moved to New York City, where she does something important in publishing. (*Pauses*) My father stayed alone for the rest of his life. He always blamed my mother for his profound unhappiness. I called him just about once a month on the phone, but I never saw him again, not face to face, until he died. (*Pauses; smiles*) Me? I got married, had a bunch of kids . . . one boy, three girls . . . all of them lovely. My wife is brilliant and strong and beautiful and I'm almost always proud of her, even though I'm also almost always jealous of other men staring at her beauty as they do. (*Smiles*) I don't know much about people really, but I do know this about myself: When the pressure's on me, my first thought is always to roar like a lion. But I try to stop myself. Mostly, I do.

(*Light fades up on Roddy [the Younger] outside house, staring in through upstage window, coldly, grimly, suspiciously . . . exactly as Archie did in earlier scenes. But then the boy smiles at Roddy [the Elder] . . . waves to him happily. Roddy [the Elder] smiles, waves back. Light fades out*)

RODDY (THE ELDER) (*to audience*): My son's a lot like me, only nicer. He never roars at all. (*Now Roddy [the Younger] enters house, goes to Molly, takes Molly's hand. Molly stops playing piano, rises from piano bench.* NOTE: Music continues without interruption. *Roddy [the Younger] and his mother dance to the music. Roddy [the Elder] watches them dance for a few moments, happily, before speaking the final words that end the play*) Like my mother used to say, "Things have got to keep changing! This is life." . . . And me, I say, "Thank God for this!"

(*Lights fade out, but for light on Molly and her son dancing. And then, after a moment, that light fades out as well. The play is over.*)

Fighting Over Beverley

"Fighting Over Beverley" had its world premiere at the Gloucester Stage Company in Gloucester, Massachusetts on August 25, 1993. It was directed by Patrick Swanson. The set was designed by Charles F. Morgan, the lighting by John Ambrosone, the costumes by Jane Alois Stein. The stage manager was James Conway. The cast was as follows:

Beverley Shimma	Judy Holmes
Archie Bennett	David Jones
Zelly Shimma	Ted Kazanoff
Cecily Shimma	Marina Re

It was subsequently produced at Stamford Theatre Works in Stamford, Connecticut. It was directed by Steve Karp. The set was designed by David Kutos, the lighting by Rob Birarelli, the costumes by Chris Lawton, the sound by Christopher A. Granger/Granger Musikwerks. The production stage manager was Debbi Roth. The cast was as follows:

Beverley Shimma	Elizabeth Wilson
Archie Bennett	George Taylor
Zelly Shimma	John Braden
Cecily Shimma	Priscilla Shanks

The People of the Play

ZELLY SHIMMA, late sixties
ARCHIE BENNETT, late sixties
BEVERLEY SHIMMA, late sixties; married to Zelly
CECILY SHIMMA, early forties; the daughter

The Place of the Play

The entire action of the play is contained in the living room of Beverley and Zelly Shimma's home, overlooking the Inner Harbor, Gloucester, Massachusetts.

The Time of the Play

Midwinter, the present. From midday of the first day until late afternoon of the next.

Sequence of Scenes

Act One
Scene One: 1 PM, Saturday.
Scene Two: 7 PM, Saturday.
Scene Three: 7:30 AM, Sunday.

Act Two
Scene One: Noon, Sunday.
Scene Two: 2 PM, Sunday.
Scene Three: 5 PM, Sunday.

For
Gillian

ACT ONE

ACT ONE

Scene One

In the darkness, we hear inspirational World War II song, "If You Love Me (I Won't Care)," sung by Vera Lynn.

Living room, Beverley and Zelly Shimma's house, Gloucester, Massachusetts; one o'clock in the afternoon. Prominent in upstage area of room, we see Hammond electric (house) organ. Center of room, we see cushioned sofa and matching overstuffed chairs.

Front door to house is located upstage left; upstage right, we see swinging door to kitchen and staircase to upstairs rooms. Upstage, we see two windows overlooking Gloucester Harbor. Outside through windows we see snow falling. It is winter, deadly cold. In the distance, the wind howls, the odd hound bays, the copious buoys sway, causing their warning bells to chime. The lighthouse foghorn bleats its endless caution; a seagull screeches out in hunger. A seasonal thunderclap sounds.

Spotlight on Beverley Shimma standing in kitchen doorway, smiling, holding china teapot. Beverley is beautiful; once a bombshell, now, simply lovely. She speaks with an accent that combines Northeast England (Yorkshire) and Gloucester, Massachusetts. She stands smiling at Archie Bennett, Englishman. Archie wears Norfolk-style jacket, striped shirt, necktie. He is white-haired, weathered; speaks with working-class English North Country accent.

BEVERLEY: If I didn't say this is a bit of a shock, seein' you at this current age of ours, Arthur, I'd be lying through my teeth. Not that you don't look well. You do: look well. You look very well, indeed. It's just that you look . . . well . . . *sixty-nine.*

(*Lights widen to include Archie. He sits on sofa, drink in hand. Outside the window, snow falls*)

ARCHIE: I can understand your bein' rocked back on your heels a bit, Bev. I can. I half-expected to still see a skinny, full-breasted 18-year-old meself. Seein' you old as you are, well . . . it is a bit of a shocker. Not that you aren't still attractive. You definitely are that: still attractive. . . . It's just that you're not eighteen any more either, are you? Quite honestly, I expected you to look like your mum when I last saw her. But thinkin' it through, Bev, I never actually knew your mum when she was any older than about *thirty-eight* or *thirty-nine!* I mean, she was a *kid* next to you and me as we are now, wasn't she?

BEVERLEY: She's just recently died, Mum.

ARCHIE: I'm sorry. The loss must be tremendous.

BEVERLEY: Mum was ninety, very nearly ninety-one.

ARCHIE: Bless her.

BEVERLEY: She wasn't actually current in my life, Mum. I mean, we didn't *make contact,* not on a day-to-day, week-to-week basis. I didn't *depend* on Mum. She was in a home for nearly twenty-five years . . .

ARCHIE: That long?

BEVERLEY: Might even have been longer.

ARCHIE: Must have been a tremendous blow, nevertheless. When me own mam died, I was totally shattered . . . quite truly *devastated.* I didn't eat right for a year. Couldn't look at red meat or cooked chicken. (*Pauses*) Influenza.

BEVERLEY: You got it?

ARCHIE: *She* got it. That what's killed her. (*Without warning*) I never married, Bev. From the time you ran off with him

. . . from the time you disappeared . . . right up til now. No wife, no other love of any solid . . . *significance.* No romance that was ever, ya know, *estimable*. Just you in my head . . . in my *memories* . . . and nobody in my bed. (*Smiles*) There's a rhyme in that: Beverley in Archie's head, and nobody in Archie's bed! . . . Now that, to me, is poetic injustice! (*Laughs*)

BEVERLEY: I . . . (*Pauses*) Are you hungry at all? Have you eaten?

ARCHIE: I et a lovely fishy soup, in a caf' just across from the train station.

BEVERLEY: Maria's . . . "seafood chowder" . . .

ARCHIE: That's it. "Seafood chowder." It was top-class. Whacking great china bowl with just about every sort of seafood you can imagine floating in the thing . . . scallops, clams, plaice, prawns. . . . It came with a quite substantial side-portion of chips, as well, with lovely crispy bits. Very nice meal, that.

BEVERLEY: One of our favorites. . . . When our daughter Cecily visits, she brings absolute buckets back with her to California, frozen in tubs. She adores Maria's chowder.

ARCHIE: Beats bangers and mash, don't it?

BEVERLEY: But, Arthur, it's only one o'clock. When did you eat lunch?

ARCHIE: I was early getting into Gloucester this mornin'.

BEVERLEY: How early?

ARCHIE: Quite early. I et both me breakfast and me lunch in town . . . before comin' here to your house.

BEVERLEY: You should've come straight here.

ARCHIE: I had a look around Gloucester.

BEVERLEY: You shouldn't've wandered about in the cold, Arthur. That was silly. You should've come straight to us. (*Pauses*) You came in by train?

ARCHIE: I did . . . but not all the way from home.

BEVERLEY (*laughing*): Well, I know that! You must have *flown* from home.

ARCHIE: I took a boat from home.

BEVERLEY: Did you? . . . A cruise ship?

ARCHIE: A freighter . . . a container ship . . . out of Liverpool.

BEVERLEY (*pouring out fresh cups of tea*): There's yours.

ARCHIE: Tar very much, lovey. (*Sips; smacks his lips*) Lovely!

(*Archie and Beverley share a smile*)

ARCHIE: I don't fly. Not since the war. It's too upsetting. I've had my fill of sky and clouds, thank you very much.

BEVERLEY: I can understand that, Arthur. I really can. Zelly doesn't like flying after his bad luck in the war.

ARCHIE: I shouldn't think he would.

BEVERLEY: Zelly has some terrible memories!

ARCHIE: As do I! I don't even try to sleep at night. My night-dreams are too upsetting. I get whatever sleep I can in the daytime. Usually, no more than an hour or two.

BEVERLEY: And that's enough? . . . Rest.

ARCHIE: Rest? Rest is something other than sleep, isn't it? (*There is a pause*) You know, Bev, I'd known Zelly'd lost his leg, but actually seeing it, actually meeting Zelly, I mean, and seeing firsthand that he's legless, I . . . well . . .

BEVERLEY: It's upsetting, I know, but Zelly's adjusted to the artificial leg totally. He takes two walks a day.

ARCHIE: Does he, then?

BEVERLEY: Two a day. One in the morning, one in the afternoon.

ARCHIE: Every morning, every afternoon?

BEVERLEY: Never misses.

ARCHIE: That's good to know, eh?

(*Archie smiles at Beverley flirtatiously. Beverley giggles girlishly*)

BEVERLEY: *Arthurrr!* (*Exits into kitchen with tea tray. Archie calls after her*)

ARCHIE: We've got things to sort out, don't we, Bev? All this chat and back-chat we're doin' is bloody tiresome. Small talk, middle talk, grand talk: it's all just bloody useless *talk*, isn't it? We don't have time! It's not like we're *young people!* (*Beverley re-enters*) Is your Zelly a good husband, then?

BEVERLEY: As husbands go, Zelly's a good one, yes.

ARCHIE (*without warning*): You made a terrible mistake, Beverley. I'm sure you know that you did. I mean, it's obvious, isn't it? (*Pauses*) I intend to take you back with me, Beverley. He's had you for forty-five years. Enough's enough, isn't it? I may not have personally married, but I know how these marriages work, Bev. Each one grows complaisant . . . mild . . . obliging. You get along, but there's no fight left, there's no fire, no passion, no . . . excitement. We'll be starting fresh, you and me, Bev. It'll fire you up. You'll live longer. I promise you.

BEVERLEY: Arthur, you can't be serious!

ARCHIE: Oh, I am, Bev. I've loved only you. At first I thought it was just a kind of obsession . . . because of your jilting me as you did. But, after some years, I came to realize it was true love, Bev. Nobody's ever held a candle to you! You're the one.

BEVERLEY (*stunned*): I'm just . . . flabbergasted!

ARCHIE: Are you now? Well then, you can easily imagine how bloody flabbergasted *I* was, can't you? . . . Waitin' at the station in Knutsford, alone, ring in a ring-box in me pocket, all paid for. Smile all over me face: ear to bloody ear! I'm watchin' couples re-couplin', kissin', huggin', passion in the air thick as mustard! I'm thinkin' ta meself, "Bev's *so in love with me!*" . . . Ten hours later, I trudge home, totally nackered, deeply depressed, bewildered, quite honestly devastated, and I hav'ta tell Mam you never showed. She is stunned. Nearly falls backwards from the shock of it. I tell her I think you've bolted with your Yank. Mam says ta me, "Never!" She says, "Bev's not that sort!" Two years later, almost to the day, that woman is in her grave.

BEVERLEY: You're not implying I was in any way *responsible* for your mum's death, are you? (*Stares at Archie. Five count*) You are.

ARCHIE: This is not a matter of implication, Miss Leach. These are hard, cold facts of life!

BEVERLEY: I was eighteen, Arthur.

ARCHIE: As was I!

BEVERLEY: I'm so sorry, Arthur. I'm sorry that I did what I did. If I were able to live my life over, I would do things differently.

ARCHIE: How so?

BEVERLEY: I wouldn't've run off so mysteriously. I would've talked with you eye-to-eye, truthfully.

ARCHIE: Would you have changed the outcome?

BEVERLEY: Meaning would I still have married Zelly?

ARCHIE: Well . . . yes.

BEVERLEY: I don't know if I would have married Zelly, but I do certainly know I wouldn't have married *you*, Arthur.

ARCHIE (*after a pause; feelings hurt*): I think I should be told why you've just said what you've just said.

BEVERLEY: Oh, Arthur . . . *please!* Entire *lifetimes* have passed between then and now. I will not be made to feel so profoundly *guilty*.

ARCHIE: No one can make a person feel guilt that isn't there, Bev. I hav'ta say this to you because it's what I deeply feel to be true. (*New tone, suddenly sweet*) Would you let me kiss you, Bev? I so much want to kiss you.

BEVERLEY: I'd prefer you didn't.

ARCHIE: For old time's sake.

BEVERLEY: I think not. (*She pauses, thoughtfully*) The idea of a man wanting to kiss me . . . wanting me romantically . . . is not an unattractive idea. And you're not an unattractive man, Arthur. But I don't mean to hold out any false hope, especially to you, given our . . . history. I only want to be truthful with you. (*Without warning*) Close your eyes, please.

(*Archie closes his eyes. Beverley kisses him on lips lightly*)

ARCHIE: I love you dearly, Bev . . .

(*Archie moves in for a major kiss. Beverley backs away. He pulls her to him roughly. She pushes him away from her angrily*)

BEVERLEY: Certainly not!

ARCHIE: Please, Bev . . .

BEVERLEY: *This is my husband's house! Kindly respect this!*

ARCHIE (*yelling; a rejected lover*): *Why did you run off and marry him?*

BEVERLEY: *Because I fell in love with him!*

ARCHIE: *Why?*

BEVERLEY: Zelly was exciting to me! He was forbidden by my parents. He was exotic, he was *American!* . . . Zelly was young and beautiful. He got into a plane and he flew against the enemy. Zelly fought to save me, my family, our little town . . .

ARCHIE: *So did I, all of the above!* What's so bloody great about what he did versus what I did?

BEVERLEY: There's a tremendous difference, Arthur. Zelly was shot down whilst protecting me . . . *us!* Zelly was decorated, made a hero. Even my father called Zelly "hero."

ARCHIE: Because he was shot down?

BEVERLEY: I beg your pardon?

ARCHIE: Him: Zelly. Gettin' shot down made the hero of him?

BEVERLEY: Of course it did.

ARCHIE: *Jesus!* That is *sickening!* That just makes me *sick.*

(*Archie moves to the window, turns his back to Beverley. He clenches his hands into fists; grinds his fists together*)

BEVERLEY: I shouldn't have said "yes" to you, Arthur. It was wrong of me to have said "yes" to you. I do apologize. I wouldn't have hurt you, not knowingly, Art, not for the world. I adored you, Artie. I just didn't ever *love you.*

ARCHIE: Then whyever did you say you'd marry me, then?

BEVERLEY: Because you asked me long before I met Zelly . . . because you persisted . . . because you wouldn't let me say otherwise . . . because you wouldn't let me say "no." (*Walks to window, looks outside, then turns to Archie again*) I've just lied to you, Arthur. I was *thrilled* when you proposed marriage to me. But you, personally, did not thrill me. Zelly, personally, did.

ARCHIE: And does he, Zelly, still thrill you now?

BEVERLEY: Thrill me now? . . . No.

ARCHIE: Then leave him, Bev! He's had his time! He's had his chance! Let me have mine! I know I can thrill you. Maybe I couldn't when I was nineteen, but I can thrill you *now* . . . and he can't now. You said so yourself! . . . We can't let the most exciting times of our lives slip so far into the past. That's death! We've got to have plans for the future! *Thrillin'* plans! We've got to find outrageous thrills! We got to have life left! Beverley, please trust me! . . . I understand that Zelly did all the right kind of talkin' ta you back then. But back then's done and gone, and it's *me* who's bloody talkin' to you *now,* my love! I'm talkin' and I'm sayin' I got me health, I've got a fair spot of wealth and I've got all the time in the world to prove the tremendous lot of love I feel for you, Beverley Leach. You're the only woman I've ever bloody loved, Beverley. And, oh, God, I do still love you. What I lack in grace and charm, I make up for in the depth of my love for you, lass. What I lack in the way I look, I make up for in the way I look at *you!* . . . Let me prove myself to you, Bev. The worst that can happen is that you'll explode yourself out of this bloody *tedium!*

(*Door slam. Zelly calls from off*)

ZELLY: I'm hommmmme!

BEVERLEY (*pulls away from Archie stiffly*): Zelly.

ARCHIE: At least he's smart enough to announce himself . . . in case we were in the throes of *Copulatas Delecto* [sic].

BEVERLEY (*astonished*): *Pardon?*

ARCHIE: Don't say "yes" or "no" now, Beverley. Just promise me you'll think about all this.

BEVERLEY (*looking away, frowning. She then turns, looks at Archie, smiles*): I'll think about all this, Arthur. I do promise you.

(*Zelly Shimma, American, enters, carrying a white plastic shopping bag. He is ruggedly handsome, probably bald; has an artificial leg; walks with a pronounced limp. He wears a storm coat, knit cap and scarf over baggy cord trousers, baggy turtleneck shirt, baggy cardigan. His accent is North Shore Massachusetts "Pahk Yo'r Cah In Hah'vid Yahd"*)

ZELLY: It's snowing again, wickid! The head of the harbor's frozen solid. Kids are skatin' on it . . . on the *ocean.* It'll kill you quick, this kinda wintah, if you don't bundle up, but it's beautiful to look at. At least I myself think it's beautiful. (*Goes to Beverley; removes cap*) So are you. (*Kisses Beverley*) My wife hates wintah. If she ever leaves me, she'll leave me in wintah! . . . (*Kisses Beverley again; pats her bottom*) The man loves his wife! . . . (*Smiles at Archie victoriously*) I hope you like seafood chowder, Alf. I brought us back a gallon of the stuff! (*Hands shopping bag to Beverley*) Put this on the stove, Mother, huh? It needs re-heatin'. (*To Archie*) Local chowder re-heats perfect. (*Archie looks at Beverley; laughs. Beverley laughs as well*) What's this? I miss something comical here? . . . Something funny about re-heatin' chowder? (*Looks at Beverley*) . . . What?

BEVERLEY: Archie's actually had a bowl of chowder already today.

ARCHIE: Nooo! Please! It was my first chowder, ever, and I loved it! Really, Zelly, I'd love another go . . . really!

BEVERLEY: Are you certain?

ARCHIE: Absolutely! It was lovely. I've never seen oversized prawns like that before . . . certainly not in a soup. We're used to the tinned prawns at home. Aren't we, Bev?

BEVERLEY: Ah yes. Terrible little salted prawns . . . tinned.

ARCHIE: "We're all just prawns in the game of life." My father used to make that joke endlessly. (*Beverley chuckles; Archie repeats joke*) "We're all just prawns in the game of life, Arthur."

BEVERLEY (*chuckling again politely*): It's rather sweet.

ARCHIE: No, you don't understand. . . . My father said that very same thing . . . "We're all just prawns in the game of life, Arthur" . . . over and over, from the time I can remember right up til he *died!* Possibly once or twice, each day! Drove me round the bleedin' *bend!*

BEVERLEY: It's still rather a sweet little joke.

ZELLY: That's a *joke?*

ARCHIE: Prawns in the game of life . . .

BEVERLEY: Prawns are shrimp, dear.

ZELLY: We're all just shrimp in the game of life is a *joke?*

BEVERLEY: I'll re-heat the chowder. This won't take a minute. (*Exits into kitchen carrying chowder in bag*)

ZELLY (*seeing reflection in mirror*): My goddam coat's still on! (*Slips out of his coat*) How's *your* mind, Alf?

ARCHIE: I was never clever in school, but I can remember things.

ZELLY: Hell of a thing, when a man's gotta look in the mirror to find out if his coat's still on! (*Walks his coat and boots to hallway coatrack, calls to Archie from upstage*) I never forget to put the goddam thing *on!* It's remembering the takin'-it-off part that's gettin' hahder. (*Zelly laughs then, crosses to liquor supply; stops, looks at wristwatch; squints at dial*) Christ! My eyes are gone, too! (*Zelly stretches his *arm out; reads wristwatch at distance*) Quarter pahst one. Normally, I'd say before supper is too early to drink, but seein' as you're *company . . .* (*Pours himself a straight whiskey*) What are you drinking these days, Arch?

ARCHIE: I'm not allowed.

ZELLY: Me, neither. (*Drinks whiskey down in one gulp*) What did you used ta drink in the old days, Arch?

ARCHIE: Spirits? I never drank spirits. I was never allowed to drink spirits.

ZELLY: Never?

ARCHIE: Not ever.

ZELLY: Not even when you were young?

ARCHIE: Definitely not then. My father was caretaker in a village convent school.

ZELLY: So your father didn't drink, either?

ARCHIE: Oh, I wouldn't go so far as to say *that!* . . . We lived in a Northern town called Knutsford. It's a little place. Everybody saw everything.

ZELLY: So nobody in the town drank?

ARCHIE: That's not what I'm sayin' at all! Half the people were half sozzled half the time. The other half of the time, the other half of the people were *completely* sozzled!

ZELLY (*sudden, explosive anger*): I can't follow nothin' comin' outta your mouth! You know this? Are you doin' this ta mock me, or what?

(*There is a substantial pause. A seagull screeches; a groaner groans. Archie looks closely at framed photographs on TV set. Then he speaks again in a pleasant tone, no trace of anger*)

ARCHIE: She's lovely, isn't she?

ZELLY: Who? Bev?

ARCHIE (*suddenly tough*): Aye, "Bev"! . . . Who in bloody hell do ya think I'm goin' on about? Pope Pius the bloody *Third?* Are you givin' me stick?

(*There is another substantial pause. Seagull screeches again; groaner groans, again. Then Zelly speaks in a most pleasant tone; no trace of anger*)

ZELLY: I'm gonna have myself another shot. Wanna join me?

ARCHIE (*gentle again*): I'll have a belt of the brandy, if it's all the same. I see your Napoleonic Brandy bottle's out for public viewin' and, one might assume, *consumption,* yes? If it's all the same to ya, I'll have a belt of that.

(*Zelly walks to liquor cabinet with pronounced limp; pours two drinks; turns, faces Archie*)

ZELLY: Here. (*Hands brandy to Archie; catches Archie staring at missing leg*) You starin' at my leg?

ARCHIE: Nooo! (*Takes glass from Zelly*) Tar, Zelly, very much . . . (*Raises glass to Zelly; recites schoolboy toast*) Hair of the dog, tooth of the rat . . . never eat flesh and you'll never grow fat. (*Downs drink*)

ZELLY (*raising glass to Archie*): Cheers . . . good health . . . may the best man win.

ARCHIE: It's the *"better"* man, not the *"best"* man. It's just two of us. Three of us and it'd be the *"best"* man. (*Pauses*) You're not implyin' there are more of us . . . other men?

(*Zelly downs his drink; never answers Archie's question*)

ZELLY: The thing I've always hated about the English is that they're always correctin' your English. I've been speakin' English just like I'm speakin' now for my whole life and nobody ever didn't know what I was sayin'. You follow me on this? (*Looks at photo of Beverley in Archie's hands*) Bev was something then, huh? How come we get so old, so fast, huh, Arch? We have all these big-deal plans . . . all these *wickid* big-deal plans . . . but then we finally get some time for ourselves, get a coupla bucks in our pocket and our wickid big-deal plans don't fit nothin'! They don't make sense for the people we are now . . . for our age. . . . It's wickid awful depressin', huh?

ARCHIE: Oh I dunno. . . . Some people think their grand plans keep 'em goin', keep 'em *alive.* Some of our deepest thinkers say, "Without grand plans, you pack it in."

ZELLY: You got yourself some *grand plans,* Arch?

ARCHIE: Oh, yes, Zelly, I most assuredly do.

ZELLY: I was thinkin' you might. (*There is a small silence*) You ready for another belt?

ARCHIE: Don't mind if I do.

(*Zelly moves toward Archie. His limp is evident. Archie stares*)

BEVERLEY (*calling from offstage*): Chowdah's ready! (*Enters smiling*) It's ready. We'll eat in the kitchen, if you don't mind. (*Exits into kitchen*)

ZELLY (*staring at Archie a moment coldly. Then, he smiles*): Soup's on. (*Raises glass in toast to Archie*) Good health, Archie. May the best man win. (*Downs drink. The lights fade to black.*)

ACT ONE

Scene Two

Later that evening. Spotlight up on Beverley at Hammond organ, playing and singing "Auf Wiederseh'n." She imitates Vera Lynn quite well, indeed. Lights widen to include Archie and Zelly. They are singing along, as well. Archie is quite drunk; happy, openly sentimental. Zelly is also quite drunk; unhappy, openly jealous of Archie.

ARCHIE: Vera Lynn was the greatest female singer what ever lived on the planet Earth.

ZELLY: She was pretty good, yuh.

(*Beverley changes tune; now sings "We'll Meet Again." Archie and Zelly chime in*)

BEVERLEY: It was an amazing time, wasn't it?

(*Beverley changes tune; now sings "Yours." Men chime in*)

ARCHIE (*weeping openly. He wipes his eyes with his handkerchief*): Oh, God bless us, it still brings tears to me eyes! I've said it once and I'll say it again: Vera Lynn was the greatest female singer what ever lived on the planet Earth!

(*Beverley continues to play organ lightly under the scene*)

ZELLY: Who da ya think the greatest male singer was, Arch?

ARCHIE: In my opinion? . . . I never liked male singers.

ZELLY: Sinatra?

ARCHIE: I certainly never liked *Sinatra.*

ZELLY: Crosby?

ARCHIE: I couldn't *bear* Crosby!

BEVERLEY: Arthur never liked any Yanks at all, did you, Arthur?

ARCHIE: Not so much, no. I found Crosby a bit repulsive after his hair went thin.

BEVERLEY: My Dad hated Yanks, til he met Zelly. When the Americans first got into the war, my Dad always useta tell me and my sisters, "Stay away from the Yanks!" . . . (*Imitates her father's voice*) "Yanks are oversexed, overpaid and over here!"

(*Zelly and Beverley share a laugh. Archie stares, stone silent*)

ARCHIE: We used ta say, "Brit rhymes with grit. Yank rhymes with wank!"

(*Archie laughs at his own small joke, loudly*)

ZELLY: Bev's dad and I got wickid close, like family. I don't mean like in-laws kinda thing. I mean like *family.*

ARCHIE (*smiling to Beverley*): I remember your dad well.

ZELLY: Bev's dad was like my best friend. Honest ta God! I wouldn't make a move without askin' Den Leach first. When I quit my job cuttin' at Gorton's and started my own fish business, I waited an extra three months, just so he could get over here first and check it out . . .

BEVERLEY: He's been gone about twenty years now . . .

ZELLY: I miss Bev's father more than I miss my own father. . . . I would've liked to have called him "Dad," honest ta Christ!

BEVERLEY: He suffered, wickid, Dad did . . .

ARCHIE: I'm sorry to hear this.

ZELLY: You wonder what God's thinkin', sometimes, makin' a man like Den Leach suffer like that. . . . The man had Heaven's Touch. I swear to Christ! When they found me, I was barely breathin' . . . they thought I was a dead man! November of '44, November twelfth . . . two dozen of Adolph's fly-boys, Heinkel III's, outta nowhere. Just six of us, mostly Mustangs. We were fighting in the clouds over the town of Beverley, Bev's mum's town . . .

BEVERLEY: I was named for Beverley.

ZELLY: . . . A buncha Spitfires come up to help . . . Brits. I got hit from behind . . . first barrage. I fell out of the sky. . . . My plane went down on Spaulding Moor, half a mile from the runway . . . exploded . . . nothin' left of it. I parachuted clear, but I was way too low for a soft touch. Both my hip joints shattered from the force of my hitting the ground. All the main nerves in this leg got cut. Bone was sticking out through the skin every-which-way. (*Pauses*) I shouldn't complain, huh? I was one of the lucky ones! My best friend, Tommy Murphy, got hit direct, blown to bits. They only found pieces of 'im. They never found his head. Eighteen years old, bright, nice, smiley kid. . . . They got me back to the base hospital and they worked on me 'round the clock. . . . They told me I was gonna live, but they hadda take my leg. That's what they told me . . . straight words, direct, no beatin' around the bush, no hedgin' any bets. . . . Five doctors in a goddam circle around me . . . all educated, trained men . . . all of 'em dead wrong! They could've grafted bone and saved it! They just did what they did 'cause it was quick! . . .

'Cause it was easy for *them!* . . . (*Pauses; sadly*) . . . Two of 'em were Americans, two of 'em were Brits, and a little Czech runt son of a bitch! . . . Educated, trained doctors, all of 'em! . . . Imagine: takin' a kid's leg when you don't have to?! . . . *Shit!* (*Zelly suddenly sobs. Beverley reaches behind her head, without turning around, grasps Zelly's hands*) Once the leg was gone, all's I wanted ta do was roll over and die! I knew I wasn't goin' home whole. . . . You know what I mean? I knew I wasn't gonna ever work no fishing boat on my own. I couldn't see any reason for staying alive! Den Leach taught me different, right off the bat. Soon as he sat down, he looked me in the eye and he goes, "Zelly-lad, I never met a Yank didn't have more piss and fight than God himself! Get off your bottom, lad, and get a move on!" . . . And he gets 'em ta strap a heavy old metal leg on me and then he shoves me out of my goddam bed! Can you imagine this? *He shoves me out of my goddam bed!* It was like God himself sent Den Leach to Zelly Shimma ta do this! Between Bev and Den, I was up and walking every day of my life from then on. They saved my miserable goddam life, that's what!

(*There is a small silence*)

ARCHIE: I was stationed just over the road, at Pocklington . . .

ZELLY: I knew this, yuh. Bev told me this.

ARCHIE: I was in the same skirmish. Twelfth November . . .

ZELLY (*after a pause*): I knew this, too, Arch, yuh.

ARCHIE: Auxiliary Squadron #608 . . . joint membership . . . us, you Yanks, Czechs, Poles . . .

ZELLY: I knew this, too.

ARCHIE: We were sergeants, gettin' thirty quid a month. You lot were lieutenants, gettin' (what?) five times that . . .

ZELLY: $255 a month, plus allowances . . . big money, back then.

ARCHIE: My point exactly . . . (*Archie pauses; remembers*) . . . A squadron of Jerries made it through . . . one bomber, two dozen Heinkels. I went up with nine others . . . Spitfires. We chased 'em off.

ZELLY: I guess you Brits'd have ta get the credit for chasin' 'em off, yuh.

ARCHIE: Terrifying thought . . . Jerries comin' in and out of England at will, like it was no trouble for 'em at all! I meself think the Irish were in cahoots with Adolph . . . thick with him, teamed up . . .

ZELLY: I never heard that particular theory myself.

ARCHIE: It's me own. I got no use for the Irish. I'd rather go to war *against* 'em than with 'em! I'll tell the God's honest: I never met an Irishman who wouldn't drink your vinegar and bugger your spaniel! (*Without warning*) Late in the war, they dropped the length of the trainin' period for RAF flyers like me from fourteen weeks down to six, but with you Yanks, they threw the bloody requirements out the *window*, didn't they? Nothin' cheered me more than watchin' your Yank "Seven-Day Wonders" tryin' ta start their engines! Throttle in one hand, bleedin' engine specs in the other! Handbooks on their laps opened to Lesson #1! And they're goin' up ta meet Adolph in the clouds! Quite a giggle! More humourous than your Bob Hope, I can tell ya fuckin' *that*, mate! (*Beverley stops playing. There is an astonished pause. Archie smiles, awkwardly*) I hope you can pardon my *français*, Bev. I shouldn't be thinkin' or talkin' about wartime. It's too upsetting. I get on about it, don't I, now? I get myself too worked up. I offer my apology.

BEVERLEY: I accept. And to Zelly?

ARCHIE: I said nothing to offend Zelly, did I? (*Archie turns, faces Zelly*) You not Irish, are you?

ZELLY: Me? Irish? Nope.

ARCHIE: Wouldn't surprise me none, if you turned out ta be, after I said what I said about the Irish. I'm always sayin' the painfully incorrect thing. I've got a bleedin' *knack!* Me dad used ta tell me I put me foot in me mouth so often, I had heel marks on the backa me throat! (*There is a moment's pause*) So, what are you then?

BEVERLEY: Zelly's half Jewish.

ARCHIE: I think I knew that from your letters. (*Smiles at Zelly*) Well now . . . half Jewish. Bein' half Jewish beats bein' *all* Jewish, doesn't it? (*Pauses*) What's the other half?

ZELLY: "Portegee," mostly, with some Italian snuck in.

ARCHIE (*happy to hear the Portuguese connection*): There you go then! (*Explains*) I had a lovely holiday in Portugal a few years back. The Portuguese do very nice fish dishes. I love a nice piece of fish. (*Smiles a conspirator's smile*) The Italian that snuck in's better left undiscussed. (*Archie laughs. There is an embarrassed pause*) Stop me, if I'm sayin' painfully incorrect things. I'm sure you can understand my desperate case of nerves, mate . . . not seein' Bev in all these years. . . . (*Pauses*) It's a tricky situation we've got goin' among us, isn't it? I don't want you to think I don't appreciate your letting me stay under your roof, Zelly, mate. I do . . . I appreciate your hospitality . . . given who you are in relation to Bev; and given who I am in relation to Bev.

ZELLY: You're welcome in my house, Archie, 'cause you're one a' Bev's oldest friends. Also, I gotta admit that Den Leach spoke well of ya, too, so that in itself is more'n enough ta let you through my door. But I'm gonna tell you som'pin, *bub!* . . . You so much as touch a finger to my wife and I'll rip you ta pieces and feed you to the fuckin' seagulls! You get me on this?

(*There is another small silence. Then Archie laughs nervously. Then Beverley resumes playing and singing "Auf Wiederseh'n" quietly*)

BEVERLEY (*singing*): ". . . We'll kiss again, Like this again. Don't don't let the teardrops start. With love that's true . . ."

(*Beverley stops playing; turns, faces the men; speaks*) I can't say it isn't flattering . . . you two . . . what's goin' on here . . . 'cause, the odd thing is, it is: flattering. But at the same time I think you're both disgusting . . . absolutely and utterly disgusting.

(*Beverley resumes playing, this time without singing. After a few moments, she bangs her fists down on to the keyboard.*

Archie and Zelly turn and face Beverley, who looks first at Zelly, then at Archie . . . then she bows her head. The lights fade to black.)

ACT ONE

Scene Three

7:30 AM, *next day. In the darkness, we hear the morning sounds of Gloucester Harbor: the straining engine of a dragger; a buoy-bell clangs; a lighthouse foghorn groans its warning; copious screeching seagulls fly past the Shimma house in search of precious food.*

Lights fade up on Archie facing Cecily Shimma. Cecily is in her 40s, looks younger. She is adorable; beautiful in the California style . . . thin and fit. In Cecily's beauty, we see Beverley's past. She probably wears all black: designer jeans, and layers of 100% cotton.

Cecily's accent is a mix of L.A. and Gloucester. There is a British influence on her speech as well. NOTE: Cecily's suitcases are in evidence in hallway, near front door.

Archie speaks to Cecily, middle of a thought.

ARCHIE: [My name is] Archie Bennett . . . (*Corrects himself*) *Arthur* Bennett.

CECILY (*almost laughing*): *You're* Arthur Bennett?

ARCHIE: The man himself!

CECILY: My Goddd! (*Cecily gives in to laughter. Archie stares at her, humiliated*)

ARCHIE: I must say, over the years, very few people have been as dead amused by that particular fact of my life as *you* seem ta be. (*Cecily giggles*) What's so funny, may I ask?

CECILY: It's just that I've been hearing about you for years . . .

ARCHIE: Have you?

CECILY: I have . . .

ARCHIE: From whom, may I ask?

CECILY (*imitating his accent*): From me mum . . . but every time she talked about you, it was always in this darkly romantic-slash-sexual context. . . . Oh God, the same thing happened when I went to a Sinatra concert when I was in college. I don't mean I got the giggles: I mean the *surprise* . . . the same kind of shock and surprise. All the time I was little, my parents went on and on about Sinatra. They played all his records, took me to a couple of his movies . . . . When I went to his concert years later, I was twenty, and it never once occurred to me that in life Sinatra'd be this old old guy, still acting young and, ya know, *cutesy*. . . . He comes out on stage and all these old ladies around me start screaming *"Frankeeeeee!"* and he tosses his jacket over his shoulder, like this . . . *impish*. . . . Then this 200-piece orchestra starts playing "Try A Little Tenderness," and Sinatra starts doin' this boyish "I love you" with his baby-blue eyes, and every old lady around me is instantly reduced to *tears*, and I don't *get* it! I mean, straight and simple, *I don't get it!* I mean, have you ever heard *Otis Redding* sing "Try A Little Tenderness"? Now, *that* is something to fucking *cry* about! . . . You know what I'm sayin' here?

(*After a small silence, Archie stares directly at Cecily. He sings a travesty of "Smoke Gets In Your Eyes" with an overstated Yiddish accent*)

ARCHIE (*singing*): "Dey asked me how I knew . . . Ginzburg was a Jew. I promptly replied . . . 'He's been circumsized' . . . Dis is how I knew . . ."

(*There is another small silence. Archie breaks it; his voice suddenly stern*) I don't give a tinker's damn *who* you are, sissy, Bev's kid or Bev herself, I don't like havin' me piss taken! You wanna try ta take the piss outta me, you're gonna be squashed! I'm the *master* of piss-takin'!

(*Beverley enters, smiling. She wears a "dress-up" dress: one that would normally be worn at night*)

CECILY: Wow! Look at *you!*

BEVERLEY (*smiling*): Thank you, dear. . . . Have you introduced yourselves?

CECILY: Sort of.

ARCHIE: Not formally.

BEVERLEY: Cecily Shimma . . . Arthur Bennett. Arthur . . . Cecily. Cecily . . . Arthur. Cecily's my daughter.

ARCHIE: She *had* to be your daughter, 'cause you're berries from the same bleedin' bush, you are!

BEVERLEY: I've mentioned Arthur to you, haven't I, dear? . . .

(*Archie laughs*)

CECILY: Did you tell Daddy?

BEVERLEY: That you're home? . . . Yes.

CECILY: And?

BEVERLEY: Well . . . he's quite upset.

CECILY: And?

BEVERLEY: Well . . . he'll tell you himself. He's just getting dressed. (*Looks at clock on wall*) Goodness me! It's still terribly early, isn't it?

CECILY: The red-eye always gets into Boston early. They say it lands at six-thirty, but, it really lands at five-thirty. If they advertised five-thirty, nobody would ever take it, so they lie. (*To Archie*) Sorry . . . I always babble when I'm sleep-deprived.

BEVERLEY (*to Archie*): It's always something, isn't it? I mean, just when you think your troubles are *this,* then, suddenly, they're *that!* . . . Cecily's left her husband.

ARCHIE: Just?

CECILY (*looking at watch*): Eight and a half hours, now. He drove me to the airport.

ARCHIE: What grounds?

CECILY: The airport?

ARCHIE: The divorce.

BEVERLEY: Are you getting *divorced?*

CECILY: On the grounds that enough is enough.

ARCHIE: I'll drink to that.

CECILY: On the grounds that men are selfish, heartless pigs. (*Imitates Archie's accent*) Do I not hear ya drinkin' to *that,* mate?

BEVERLEY: Are you getting *divorced,* Cecily?

CECILY: I dunno.

BEVERLEY: What did you tell Arthur? Why did Arthur say what he said?

CECILY: He's *your* boyfriend, not mine. Ask him.

ARCHIE: I've known many a married man and wife to live separate from one another for years and years, but never actually divorce. Better for the kiddies, they say. If you don't mind me givin' ya a spot of advice, that'd be it, Sicily [sic] . . . live separate, but never divorce.

CECILY: Did you call me *Sicily?* My name's not Sicily. It's *Cecily.*

ARCHIE: Oh, is it? Sorry, love. I thought your name was Italian. Your Dad said some Italian snuck into the family.

CECILY: You mean snuck in like through the *window* kind of thing? (*To Beverley*) What's he saying?

BEVERLEY: I don't know! (*To Archie*) What are you saying exactly, Arthur?

ARCHIE: I thought you'd said you'd given your daughter an Italian name.

CECILY: *Sicily?* You thought my parents named me *Sicily?*

ARCHIE: I've known of many a Swiss-miss to be named Geneva.

(*There is a small pause as Cecily, confused, rolls her eyes heavenward*)

CECILY: It must be the time-change. (*To Archie; explains*) I'm still on L.A. time.

BEVERLEY (*brightly; to Cecily*): Arthur's still on *English* time! It's already *afternoon* in Arthur's mind! He's six hours ahead of us!

CECILY: That explains it. By lunchtime, I'll know what he's talking about.

BEVERLEY (*brightly; to Archie*): Cecily's been living out in California. She's in the entertainment industry.

CECILY: I made this terrible career choice. I misheard my father. I thought he told me to go into *show* business. It turns out he'd told me to go into the *shoe* business. Of course, he also told me *The Lion, The Witch, And The Wardrobe* was *really* called "The Lying *Bitch* In The Wardrobe"! You boys do have your little prejudices, eh?

ARCHIE (*glaring at Cecily, suspicious that he's the butt of her small jokes*): Is it just California men you find to be piglike or is it *all* men you find to be piglike?

CECILY: Only a man would have to ask.

(*After a small pause, Beverley leaps in to save the moment*)

BEVERLEY: Cecily's a very successful talent agent. She represents film directors and screenwriters. Her husband's a screenwriter. He's working on a screenplay with George Harrison, the former Beatle.

ARCHIE: The singing Beatles? From up home?

BEVERLEY: Not all of them. Just the one: George.

(*Zelly enters the room*)

CECILY: Hi!

ZELLY: Who's with Little Gerald?

CECILY: That's not my problem.

ZELLY: Fine.

(*Zelly exits into kitchen*)

ARCHIE: Is your husband not very tall, then?

CECILY: What?

BEVERLEY (*smiling; explains*): Little Gerald's her stepson.

CECILY: He's with his mother.

BEVERLEY: He's nine.

ARCHIE: He's *yours?* Not hers?

BEVERLEY: Pardon?

ARCHIE: You said "Little Gerald is mine" . . .

BEVERLEY: *Nine!* I said "Little Gerald is *nine*"!

ARCHIE: Me hearin's gettin' worse and worse. (*Cecily laughs. Archie snaps at her; annoyed*) You're not one of these nutter feminists I've been reading about, are you? Hairy legs and armpits . . . feminists can't stay married more than a matter of weeks! Both of the Queen's pathetic sons married feminists, didn't they? Is that what you are, then, a bleedin' feminist?

(*Wordlessly, Cecily shows Archie her armpit, just as Zelly reenters from kitchen carrying mug of coffee. Zelly sees Cecily's arm in the air*)

ZELLY: What are you doing?

CECILY (*imitating Archie's Northern accent*): Nuthin' much, Dad. I'm just showing Archie me hairy armpit.

ZELLY: *What?* (*There is a small embarrassed silence. Zelly turns to Cecily*)

ZELLY: Take a walk with me.

CECILY: Outside? . . .

ZELLY: Yes, outside . . .

CECILY: It's snowing!

ZELLY: So what?

CECILY: My blood's thinner than yours!

BEVERLEY: They say this happens to East Coast people after they've lived in California a while: they become cold-blooded.

CECILY (*laughing*): It's the essential nature of the film industry.

BEVERLEY: I beg your pardon, dear?

CECILY: Cold-bloodedness.

BEVERLEY: The *climate!* . . . I mean the climate . . . (*To Archie; smiling; chirping nervously*) I meant the climate. . . . When easterners go west, they get cold. Their blood thins . . .

(*Suddenly, Zelly yells at Beverley*)

ZELLY: Stop your goddam babble, will you?! You're makin' a fool of yourself! . . . You sound *stupid!*

(*There is a hideous pause*)

CECILY: Nice. Really nice.

ARCHIE: Would you like me to take a walk then, Zelly? I wouldn't mind, mate. I rarely see a snowstorm as violent as this one. I'd like very much to be out experiencing it firsthand.

BEVERLEY: Noooo . . .

ZELLY: Yuh, that'd be great. We need to have a family pow-wow.

BEVERLEY: Meeting, he means.

ARCHIE: I know what "powwow" means . . . from the pictures.

BEVERLEY (*to Zelly*): He means the movies.

ZELLY (*angrily*): I know what he means!

BEVERLEY: I'll walk with you, Arthur. We could get the morning paper.

ARCHIE: Lovely.

BEVERLEY (*to Zelly*): It'll give you two a few minutes alone.

ARCHIE: I'll leave you lot, then. (*To Beverley*) I'll have to borrow some boots.

BEVERLEY: Let me see your foot . . . (*Looks*) Zelly's spare snowboots should fit you. They're in the pantry. We'll go out the back door. (*To Zelly*) Don't be angry with her without listening. Listen to her side first.

ZELLY: Fine.

BEVERLEY (*kissing Cecily*): Don't be hostile toward your father, dear. He only wants the very best for you. (*And then she kisses Zelly*) Is a half hour enough?

ZELLY: Fine.

BEVERLEY: Come with me, Arthur.

(*Beverley and Archie exit into the kitchen*)

CECILY: He's disgusting!

ZELLY: Don't change the subject!

CECILY: It's not your life, it's *my* life!

ZELLY: Oh yuh? Whose house are you stayin' in?

CECILY: You want me to leave? Fine! Now? Tonight? When?

ZELLY: What about Little Gerald?

CECILY: What *about* Little Gerald? He's got a mother and a father! (*Suddenly*) Doesn't it ever occur to you to put your arms around me and say, "I can see you're unhappy and I love you!"?

ZELLY: Doesn't it ever occur to you to call yo'r motha and yo'r fatha first and say, "I love you and I need you . . ." and then maybe *ask*, "Can I come to your house?" *before* you show up?

CECILY: You think I should *ask permission* to see my own mother and father? You think this house is your house, not my house, too?

ZELLY: Yuh, lady, that's what I think!

CECILY: You are really fucked up!

ZELLY: Save the gutter language for your sophisticated show-business friends! (*Pauses*) If I was forty, I'd never run home to my mother and father like I was twelve!

CECILY: That's what I started out telling myself . . . but then I thought, "uh-uh . . . you get one mother and one father and they hav'ta count . . . They hav'ta figure into your life-decisions . . .

ZELLY: Come off it! You're not lookin' for your mother and me ta help you decide nothing! You're just looking for us to back you up, no matter what bullshit you pull!

CECILY: So, is that like *a bad thing?* I mean, aren't parents s'pose ta be behind their children, no matter what?

ZELLY: Children, maybe! Forty-year-olds, hell, no! Marriage #1, fine! Marriage #2, *maybe!* Marriage #3, you're on your own, lady! Leave us out of it! You want help with a life decision, fine, here's help with a life decision: Go back to Gerald and Little Gerald and stay married. (*Pause. Cecily goes to brandy bottle, pours herself a drink*) When did you start drinking brandy in the morning?

CECILY: I'm still on L.A. time.

ZELLY: Yuh, so, that makes it even *earlier*.

CECILY: Fine. This is my last drink of the night in L.A. Cheers! (*Drinks brandy; winces*) That was just awful! . . . They say every man in France gets up in the morning, has a belt of brandy and hits his wife. Now I know why.

ZELLY: Did Gerald hit you?

CECILY: No, Gerald didn't hit me. Believe it or not, there's more to hurt than sticks and stones.

ZELLY: Let me tell you something, loud and clear, lady: I never asked for kids. I never wanted 'em and, to tell the God's honest truth, I still don't. But I got 'em, didn't I? I got you and you got me and we're stuck with each other. So this is life and we put up with each other. We make the best of it. . . . But so help me God, I'm not gonna just stand back smilin', while you mess up some innocent little nine-year-old kid!

CECILY: Like *you* did?

ZELLY: What's that crack s'pose ta mean?

CECILY: Remember me? I was the nine-year-old kid sleepin' in the pink room and *I'm* messed up! . . . Dr. Weingarten thinks I can't stay married to Gerald or anybody because of you, because of the marriage I grew up watching. . . . I'm the only person Dr. Weingarten's ever met in his entire career who actually spent their childhood praying that their parents would get *divorced.*

ZELLY: Is that a true fact?

CECILY: That is a fucking true fact! . . . Your wife is miserable, you know this? Your wife has been unhappy for forty-five years. She has felt unwanted and unloved. She has felt homesick, disconnected from everything she loved. She's wearing dresses, again, in the daytime . . . and she is panting with excitement now that that sub-humanoid's here in the house, back in her life. You know why? I'll tell you why. It's 'cause finally she's feeling some connection to her youth! Finally, she's feeling some connection to *affection!* For the first time in forty-five years, she feels *loved!*

(*Zelly shoves Cecily backwards. She falls on to sofa*)

ZELLY: *Shut your mouth!*

(*There is an astonished pause. Archie appears in kitchen doorway wearing outlandishly bright-colored snowboots*)

ARCHIE: I don't mean to interrupt. I just want to tell you that we're off now . . . Bev and me . . . into the fresh snow. (*Pauses; smiles, happily*) I'm really very happy that I spent me time and money taking this trip. *Very* happy.

(*Archie smiles. Cecily and Zelly stare at Archie and then turn and face one another. The lights fade to black.*)

ACT TWO

ACT TWO

Scene One

Noon, the same day. In the darkness, we hear recording of Vera Lynn singing "When I Grow Too Old To Dream."

Lights fade up in living room. Cecily and Beverley sit in separate chairs, eating dinner from plates on their laps. The TV is playing soap opera, opposite them, sound off.

Music fades out.

CECILY: He's nuts. You know this, yes?

BEVERLEY: Your father?

CECILY: Both of 'em! (*Eats*) They weren't talking to each other at all at breakfast, so I asked him . . . Archie . . . if he was enjoying America . . .

BEVERLEY: Oh, I think he is. What did he say?

CECILY: He said, "Yank rhymes with Wank"!

BEVERLEY: *Did* he? Again?

CECILY: And then Daddy goes, "Brit rhymes with shit"!

BEVERLEY: Dear me! They're not getting on at all well, are they?

CECILY: So, then, Archie goes, (*Imitating Archie's accent*) "That's bloody grand talk comin' from a yob who's got one leg missing!" . . .

BEVERLEY: Goodness me! Arthur *said* that?! I am *shocked!*

CECILY: For a coupla seconds, I thought they were going to have a fistfight!

BEVERLEY: I dare *say!*

CECILY: They are both terminally *nuts!* Neither of 'em said another word after that! (*Eats*) How could you even *know* somebody like that?

BEVERLEY: Arthur?

CECILY: Jesus, Mum, yes: Arthur!

BEVERLEY: It's sometimes difficult to determine which man you're so intensely hating, Cecily. You seem to hate them all.

CECILY: I'm just a little vulnerable at the moment, Mum. So maybe you could hold your more intensely judgmental thoughts to yourself.

BEVERLEY: And you can't imagine *you're* being judgmental calling both my husband and my old friend "terminally nuts"?

CECILY: I'm not judging you. I'm judging them.

BEVERLEY: Are we saying that judgement is defined objectively versus subjectively?

CECILY: Don't get British on me, Mother. Stay mid-Atlantic so we can keep talking. (*Paces nervously*) I'm either premenstrual or pre-migraine. I don't like my choices.

(*Cecily checks to see if the portable telephone is working*)

BEVERLEY: Is it working?

CECILY: *It* is. I'm not. (*Checks the clock: time of day*) Why does he sleep in the *daytime?*

BEVERLEY: Arthur? . . . Perhaps he's jet-lagged.

CECILY: He can't be jet-lagged. He came on a boat.

BEVERLEY: I suppose it's because he's unable to sleep in the nighttime. (*Explains*) He has bad dreams.

CECILY: If Archie Bennett didn't have bad dreams, I wouldn't believe in God. (*Lights a cigarette. Puffs. Suddenly jams cigarette out in ashtray*) Jesus! (*Paces*) I lived with a drummer like that for about six months. Did you ever meet Chick? He couldn't sleep in the nighttime either. It was *Proustian:* as soon as there was a crack of daylight under the bedroom door, Chick would start snoring. I'd get up for work and leave him sleeping.

BEVERLEY: I remember the name Chick from your letters, dear, but, I'm quite certain I never actually *met* your Chick.

CECILY: He was nice to me and great looking, but he used to lie awake in bed all night, worrying about everything . . . drumming his fingers on the night table . . . I didn't get a night's sleep for six fucking months!

BEVERLEY: Mind your language, dear.

CECILY (*pacing*): Where's Daddy? He knows I'm only staying one day.

BEVERLEY: He's just having his walk. You could have gone with him. He would have greatly enjoyed your company.

CECILY: It's too cold . . . and I'm too jet-lagged to put up with his harangue. I'm exhausted.

BEVERLEY: Take a nap.

CECILY: I can't sleep in the daytime. (*Stands*) I have to call my office. (*Goes to phone*) It's Saturday. (*Returns to chair;*

sits; looks at TV) What's this? What are we watching? What is this "dreck"?

BEVERLEY: I have no idea. You turned the television on, not I.

CECILY: I did? . . . I think you're right. You mind if I turn it off?

BEVERLEY: Not at all.

(*Cecily switches off TV; goes to window; looks outside*)

BEVERLEY: You seem quite overwrought, darling.

CECILY: You're *under*wrought! . . . How is it you're so calm?

BEVERLEY: Why shouldn't I be calm?

CECILY: It should be obvious what your old friend wants here.

BEVERLEY: He wants me to leave your father and move back to England with him.

CECILY: Holy shit!

BEVERLEY: Language, darling, please!

CECILY: Does Daddy know this?

BEVERLEY: He *suspects* this. He doesn't know this.

CECILY: Daddy will kill this guy if he finds out. (*Considers this; laughs*) Are you gonna?

BEVERLEY: Tell Daddy?

CECILY: *Leave* Daddy.

(*There is a pause*)

BEVERLEY: I haven't decided.

CECILY (*whispered shock*): *What?*

BEVERLEY (*standing*): I'm going to put the kettle on. I won't be a minute.

(*Beverley exits into the kitchen. Cecily goes to portable telephone, dials a number; waits; speaks to an answering machine*)

CECILY: Dr. Weingarten, this is Cecily Shimma again. I'm sorry to leave so many messages, but I'm having sort of a crisis. I'm still in Massachusetts at my parents' house. I've left you the number here in my last couple of messages, but in case your machine's broken, I'm at 508-281-4099. Please call me as soon as possible. . . . Thanks, Dr. Weingarten. I'm sorry to bother you, but I guess you know I wouldn't if I didn't feel I had to. . . . I hope your wrist is feeling better. Bye.

(*Archie enters from upstairs. He is wearing a c.1940s bathrobe. There is a white towel around his neck . . . and a small black, red and gold metallic label stuck to the center of Archie's forehead*)

ARCHIE: Oh, hullo.

CECILY: Hi. Sleep?

ARCHIE: A bit.

(*Cecily stares at the label on Archie's forehead*)

ARCHIE: Something on me head?

CECILY: There is, actually . . . some kind of label's stuck to your forehead.

ARCHIE (*finding the label; matter-of-factly*): Oh yuh, it's the label from me soap. Cussons' Imperial Leather. It's been me brand for more'n sixty years now. It was me Dad's brand and his Dad's before *him.* I wouldn't dare wash meself without Imperial Leather! The scent suits me. (*Sniffs the label*) Lovely! There's a lifetime of memories in that scent. (*Smiles at Cecily*) The label usually sticks pretty solid to the center of the bar, first three or four scrubbings. After that, it goes loose with the suds. I've found 'em in me mornin' scrambled'n'Spam more than once. You never quite know *where* they're gonna turn up! (*Without pause*) Is your dad around?

CECILY: Why?

ARCHIE: It's nothing special.

CECILY: He's out walking. Anything I can help you with?

ARCHIE: Actually, the lav I'm using upstairs is out of loo rolls.

CECILY: What's this?

ARCHIE: Do you have any loo rolls in the house?

CECILY: You mean like his old records or tapes kinda thing?

ARCHIE: I beg your pardon?

(*Beverley re-enters from the kitchen*)

BEVERLEY: Hello, Arthur. Did you sleep?

ARCHIE: A bit . . .

BEVERLEY: You're just in time for a cup of tea.

CECILY: He wants something.

BEVERLEY: And what would that be, Arthur?

ARCHIE: Do you have any spare loo rolls in the house? There's none in the upstairs lav.

BEVERLEY: In the vanity cupboard under the sink.

(*Cecily laughs*)

ARCHIE: I'm afraid I've looked there already.

BEVERLEY: Then try the en-suite lav in my bedroom. There should be a few spare loo rolls there.

ARCHIE: Thank you.

(*Archie exits upstairs. Cecily laughs again. Beverley smiles*)

BEVERLEY: Did you and Arthur have a misunderstanding?

CECILY: Arthur *is* a misunderstanding! . . . We had a mid-Atlantic language breakdown. I thought he was after Lou Rawls music which is, in my book, absolute shit. He was after toilet paper. Well, at least, Archie and I are in the same ballpark.

BEVERLEY: You're so American, darling. It still amazes me. When you were little, it was amusing: having an American child. Somehow I always thought I'd take you home, bring out the English in you. But I never did, did I? Makes me sad, really. . . . You look like me . . . like I did at your age . . . but somehow I can never find myself in anything you *say!* . . . I'm losing my Englishness myself. I mean, listen to me: I don't sound English and I don't sound American either. I don't know what I am, anymore, really. It's a bit sad, isn't it? What I mean is, well, something's lost, isn't it? . . . (*We hear tea kettle's whistle, off*) I won't be a minute.

(*Beverley exits into the kitchen. Cecily dials another number, talks to another answering machine*)

CECILY: Gerald, it's me. I'm still at my parents. I know why I'm crazy, Gerald . . . Hullo? . . . (*New tone suddenly. She is no longer talking to an answering machine*) Gerald? Hiiii! . . . Are you still sleeping? . . . I'm sorry! . . . No, no, no, go back to sleep. Call me when you get up. I'm at my parents. I'll talk to you later. Go back to sleep. . . . What? . . . Is somebody there? . . . No, I just thought I heard somebody. . . . Fine. No, no, it's fine. . . . Bye, Gerald.

(*Cecily switches portable phone off. She is terribly sad. Beverley re-enters, carrying tea tray*)

BEVERLEY: Did someone call?

CECILY: No. I called someone. (*Tries not to say more, but does*) I called Gerald.

BEVERLEY: That's a good idea. (*Puts tea tray down*) And how is Gerald?

CECILY: In bed with somebody.

BEVERLEY: Somebody? . . . Oh. I see. He told you this?

CECILY: I could hear.

BEVERLEY: Did you ask him?

CECILY: Mother, I could hear.

BEVERLEY: Sometimes when you're overwrought, dear, the imagination plays tricks . . .

CECILY: Mum, *please!*

(*Cecily fights back tears. She goes to window; looks out at the storm. Suddenly tears overwhelm her. Beverley watches her daughter weep. She keeps her distance. When she speaks, she speaks quietly*)

BEVERLEY: Are you alright, darling?

CECILY: I'm fine, Mum.

BEVERLEY: Is Gerald treating you badly?

CECILY: Yes. No. Yes.

BEVERLEY: Do you want to end your marriage?

CECILY: No. Yes. Those two things: No and yes.

BEVERLEY: Is little Gerald difficult?

CECILY: That's not it.

BEVERLEY: *What's* it, dear?

CECILY: Why do we let them get away with it, Mum? (*Pauses; explains*) Men. They can't bear any success we have, can they?

BEVERLEY: Things were different in my day, I suppose. Women didn't seem to want so much.

CECILY: You *didn't*, Mum? You always wanted to spend your life waiting for your husband to come home stinking of fish and female fish-packers? Waiting for him to come in from his homo nights out with The Boys, stinking of bar-bimboes and beer? . . .

BEVERLEY: You have such a unpleasant way of putting things, dear!

CECILY: Yuh, well, maybe I do. Maybe I'm not telling you the honest-to-God truth, Mum. Maybe it's not just daddy. Maybe it's that I'm terrified of ending up like you.

BEVERLEY: That's charmingly put, as well.

CECILY: You know what I mean, Mum! Not you, personally! You, personally, are my *ideal!* You're beautiful, witty, composed, clear-headed. . . . It's you, *married,* that terrifies me. I see what they're like, Mum . . . and I see what I'm like . . . what *we're* like. We're weak in their presence. We . . . (*Suddenly sobs; turns away from Beverley*) Shit!

BEVERLEY: Are you alright, dear?

CECILY: Never better. (*Goes to Kleenex box; dries eyes, blows nose*) I know women who used to be vital, brilliant thinkers . . . leaders . . . *world-beaters.* They had everything, except a husband and kids. So they got married, got the husband, got the kids, got the big house, closed the door behind them and never saw daylight again! I can't do this.

BEVERLEY: That's not necessarily been my life thus far, Cecily.

CECILY: What has necessarily been your life thus far, Mum? Staying alone in this goddam house day after day, waiting for him to come and go, when and if he wants? . . . What kind of life are you having?

(*There is a pause*)

BEVERLEY: I had you. . . . Your father let me go to school . . .

CECILY: Your husband *let you* go to school? You needed his *permission?*

BEVERLEY: It took money.

CECILY: Salem Teachers College took money? How much money? Five hundred a year? A thousand? Two thousand? Ten thousand?

BEVERLEY: That wasn't the issue, Cecily.

CECILY: What wasn't the issue?

BEVERLEY: Whether I worked and earned money or whether I went to school and earned no money. Your father wanted me to go to school. He was proud of me.

CECILY: You believe that?

BEVERLEY: Yes, I do believe that.

CECILY: Did he ever actually "let you" *teach* school? Did he ever actually "let you" go out of this house for fifteen minutes without your having to make a full report? Did he ever actually "let you" take a breath of air without asking his *permission?*

BEVERLEY: We're different people, you and I. I tend to look on the brighter side of things. No marriage is easy, Cecily. Your father and I have had some lovely times together.

CECILY: He bullies you. He badgers you. He treats you like you're dumb and useless. He talks down to you. He expects you to listen to the same stupifyingly boring stories, over and over, again, ten thousand times! . . . He expects you to clean up after his endless mess. And he expects you to put up with the unspeakable . . .

BEVERLEY: I must ask you to stop, now . . .

CECILY: *And he expects you to put up with the unspeakable . . .*

BEVERLEY: *Cecily, stop talking! You are insulting me! . . .*

(*Beverley sobs. Cecily goes to her, kneels at her feet, holds Beverley's hand*)

CECILY: Come away with me, Mum.

BEVERLEY: Pardon?

CECILY: I want you to come away with me.

BEVERLEY: On a holiday?

CECILY: On a *life!* . . . I want you to come back to California with me.

BEVERLEY: What are you saying, Cecily?

CECILY: I'm not going back to Gerald. I want you to come live with me, Mum. I make a lot of money. A *wickid awful* lot of money. Plenty for both of us and then some! (*Pauses*) California is warm. People are happy there . . . polite. They smile at you. They stop their cars at crosswalks! (*Pauses*) It's like the walking dead here, Mum. Everything's frozen, covered with ice. There's no work. People are broke, depressed. Gloucester's a dead place. You're married to a fisherman who doesn't fish. He limps around here, shouting orders at you like you're some dumb lumper workin' his crew. He's *got* no crew. He's got no *hope.* He's just waiting to die. You're young enough to live still, Mum. In ten more years, who knows? . . . Leave with me, Mum. Do the exciting thing for yourself. Leave him. Come live with *me!*

BEVERLEY: Why do you hate your father so?

CECILY: Because I have been in psychoanalysis for fifteen years trying to sort through my nightmares . . . trying to find a way to stop believing that every man I meet isn't really, deep-down, a woman-hating murderer come to kill me.

BEVERLEY: Oh, darling Cecily! Surely you can't blame your father!

CECILY: I can and I do! Come away with me, Mum. We're both still young enough. *You're* still young enough! . . . You can't seriously consider either one of them, Mum! They're mean and they're old. . . . In five years' time, they'll both be wearing pacemakers and colostomy bags! And you'll be wearing a nurse's uniform! Come with me, Mum! *Live* with me!

ARCHIE (*off; from the staircase*): An English nose can smell a good cuppa tea through a stone wall! (*Archie re-enters living room, smiling. He has changed his clothes; now wears a dapper suit and tie: an Englishman on holiday. He instantly senses Cecily's upset*) Am I interrupting somethin'?

(*The telephone rings*)

CECILY: It's probably for me . . . (*Cecily answers the telephone*) Hello? . . . Hiiii! (*To Beverley*) It's for me. I'll go in the kitchen.

(*Cecily exits into kitchen with portable phone. Beverley smiles at Archie*)

BEVERLEY: Don't you look smart?

ARCHIE: Marks and Sparks. Thank you very much.

BEVERLEY: Cuppa tea?

ARCHIE: Don't mind if I do.

BEVERLEY: You seem a bit more rested.

ARCHIE: I am, Bev, thank you. Very much so. (*Takes teacup from Beverley*) Tar very much, lovey. (*Archie sips tea; smacks lips*) Lovely! (*Moves closer to Beverley; looks in her eyes; smiles*) I was dreamin' about ya through my whole sleep. And it were very pleasant stuff I dreamed, as well! . . .

BEVERLEY: Oh, that *does* embarrass me.

ARCHIE: Does it, then? Good. (*Another sip*) Your girl's upset, isn't she?

BEVERLEY: I'm afraid she is.

ARCHIE: She's a bit passé ta be goin' on about men holding women back from success and all, wouldn't you say? Did she never hear of Mrs. Thatcher, then?

BEVERLEY: Were you eavesdropping?

ARCHIE: Not intentionally.

BEVERLEY: How much?

ARCHIE: Not much. It weren't all that interestin' ta me.

BEVERLEY: Cecily's very successful out in California.

ARCHIE: What's the point of her bein' very successful, if it brings her nothin' but misery?

BEVERLEY: I suppose . . .

ARCHIE: I *know.* Look at your singing Beatles her hubby's making moving pictures with. Back home, they made bloody *heroes* of 'em. They're still a whacking great *industry!* Tour guides takin' tourists to their bleedin' *haunts!*

And what's that about, really? The four of them are all misery personified! Livin' in America . . . injecting drugs, studying bizarre religions with opportunist [sic] Pakistanis! Success? One of 'em got himself shot dead in New York City, didn't he? And they're still playin' his music on the radio, aren't they? I mean, that *is* success, isn't it? But the posh wanker's still bloody dead, isn't he, eh? So, what did success do for the Beatles in the end, tell me? I'll tell you, Bev . . . in a word . . . *nothin'!* (*Downs tea; smiles at Beverley*) I'm ready for another cuppa tea, thank you . . . (*Hands cup to Beverley*) . . . So, why's the girl sniveling, really? She's had a row with her hubby, I expect. If she weren't livin' in such a posh manner, as she is, she'd have to face up to whatever's goin' wrong, wouldn't she? Instead, what's she doin' ta solve her problems? I'll tell ya: she's on a jet, flyin' home to Mum. So what's money doin' for the girl in the end, Bev? It's not solvin' her problems, is it? It's just feedin' the coffers of the bloody airlines! And that's as far as I see it. I'd personally rather be dead than be posh, and that's the truth! (*Takes cup of tea from Beverley*) Tar very much, lovey. (*Sips tea; smacks his lips*) Lovely! . . .

BEVERLEY: Are you still working, Arthur?

ARCHIE: Earning wages?

BEVERLEY: Yes . . . that, too.

ARCHIE: No. Not for more than twenty years now.

BEVERLEY: I'd wondered.

ARCHIE: Twenty-five years, one job. That's bloody enough, wouldn't you say? . . .

BEVERLEY: I suppose . . .

ARCHIE: . . . My father always used ta say, "You can't be floatin' about. Life's too short. One job and one woman: that's all a man gets."

BEVERLEY: I suppose . . .

ARCHIE: I bloody *know!* I hated my job, by and large, but a job's only a job, isn't it? I stuck with it for bloody forty years, didn't I? I've never been the sort to whinge. I'm a sticker. You'd be amazed how many of the old lads are in their graves or pokin' one toe in already! Me best mate, Rod? Dead from drink. Alfie Bottoms, the one whose aunt met King George? Hit by the bus he was runnin' to catch! So sozzled, he thought he was behind the thing! He run into the front of it, full gallop! You remember Reg Farley and Rog Montgomery? Bo'sun Menges? Nobby Smythe? All pushin' up the daffodils. From what, you may wonder? From *hopelessness.* Things is tough back home, Beverley. There's no work. There's this bloody Labour Council, but there's no bloody labour! It's a bleedin' paradox, isn't it? So they give up hope, one by one, and they die from the want of it! . . . Not me. I always had me hope, haven't I then, lovey? Just before I left me job, I heard Mrs. Thatcher herself givin' a speech to the executives at the works. I wasn't in the audience exactly . . . I was doin' my normal custodial duties . . . cleanin' up . . . but I could hear her loud and clear. She talked about the stock market and investing in England. I listened hard. I thought about what was goin' on up North, and I said to meself, "Artie, you gotta learn ta play the game by Mrs. Thatcher's rules, not by some Labour loser's rules!" And I bloody did! It were Mrs. T herself who made me wealthy! I withdrew all me pension money and I invested it in the stock market . . . but always based on Mrs. T's moves. Wherever Mrs. Thatcher went, I bet me quid on her. If she visited the Electrolux plant, I bought shares in Electrolux. If I saw a picture of her Hooverin' her bleedin' carpet, I bought Hoover. If she drank a cup of cocoa, I bought cocoa futures! . . . I stayed in the market for three years with profits soaring every day. But then, Bev, one Thursday night without warning, I had the vision. Now I must tell ya that when I was a lad, me dad used ta say, "Arthur-lad, you must never live a gambler's life. Gamblers don't gamble ta win: they gamble ta *lose!* . . . And sooner or later gamblers get their wish and lose everything they have!" I remembered his words every day whilst I was rakin' in the profits. . . . It kept me in a sweat. But this particular night, I actually had a *vision* of me dad . . . a dream in which he appeared in front of me, vividly, sayin' what he'd always said ta me about the gambler's life . . . but, this time, he ended his advice by screamin', "Sell, Arthur, sell!" It were terrifying! I screamed out loud . . . woke meself up! . . . Once I calmed down a bit, I said to meself, "Artie, you've made yourself a 2,000% profit. It's bloody *enough!* Get out! Do what Da says: Sell!" As soon as nine AM Friday mornin' rolled around, I rolled outta me bed and phoned ta me broker, Mr. Charles Peabody. I sold every investment I had. Liquified me assets. I made meself a hundred and nineteen thousand quid, after taxes . . . clear profit.

BEVERLEY: Oh, that is *wonderful*, Artie!

ARCHIE: "Wonderful" is a colossal understatement, woman! You do know what happened, seventy-two hours later, don't you, love?

BEVERLEY: The market crashed?

ARCHIE: Crashed? It fell in a hole! The papers called it "Black Monday."

BEVERLEY: I remember this . . .

ARCHIE: For me, Beverley, "Black Monday" was the golden payoff. Property values all over Britain went spiralin' down, interest on savings shot up. There are certainly richer men than I, but I am comfortable, Bev . . . very,

very, *very* comfortable. I bought meself a very substantial freehold property not far from Tatton Park . . . detached, four bedrooms, a double garage, a whacking great garden, with a small pond . . .

BEVERLEY: Oh, I love a fish pond.

ARCHIE: It's not a fish pond, woman . . . it's actually a *pond.*

BEVERLEY: How wonderful for you, Artie.

ARCHIE: It's so lovely, when me neighbors sold, they advertised that their cottage overlooked a beauty spot!

BEVERLEY: Did they?

ARCHIE: They did. (*Archie stops talking; turns, faces Beverley. He smiles at her, wordlessly for a moment*) I credit you, Beverley Leach, for every speck of me good fortune.

BEVERLEY: Me? Whyever for?

ARCHIE: Since the day I met you, Bev, I've always had the reason for livin'. And since the day I lost you, I've had the need to figure out what it was gonna take . . . to get you back. I've dedicated my life to this . . . to you.

BEVERLEY: Are you serious?

ARCHIE: Deadly so! I always knew it was gonna take some money . . . and probably a house . . . and probably my hoppin' up the class ladder a rung or two.

BEVERLEY: All these years . . . thinking of me?

ARCHIE: Some many years back, I found a great and perfect love: a true love. And this true love sustained me . . . sustained me hopes and me life. No matter how you've responded to me or how you *will* respond to me, I love you, Bev. Nothin's gonna change that. (*Archie reaches out and touches Beverley's cheek ever so gently. Beverley allows his touch*) When you used ta sing Vera's songs to me, Bev . . . I was never happier. I believed you. I believed every word.

BEVERLEY: They were just songs, Artie.

ARCHIE: But I believed them, Bev. They gave me such a thrill . . . such thrillin' hope.

BEVERLEY: We were young, Arthur. The bombs were falling.

ARCHIE (*singing a snatch of wartime song, then speaking*): That's what I remembered all these years. It's kept me goin', Beverley . . . It's kept me young.

BEVERLEY (*weeping*): Oh, dear . . . look at us . . .

ARCHIE: You're weepin', Bev.

BEVERLEY: Yes. I know. (*Laughs*) It's so sad . . . us, grown old as we have. (*Weeps again, laughs again*) Bein' young and beautiful, with bombs fallin' . . . (*Suddenly sobs*)

ARCHIE: What is it?

BEVERLEY: We should have died then, Artie. All of us. They were the lucky ones, really, the ones that loved and died. The ones that loved and lingered, like us . . . grown old. . . . We build nothing but our memories, Arthur. And then we die. And our memories die with us. It's like we never happened! It's so sad. It's such a tragic loss! . . .

ARCHIE: You don't mean what you're sayin', love!

BEVERLEY: I'm sure I don't. I'm sure you're right. There must have been some lovely moments, afterwards . . . with my family. But, what? I can't remember what.

ARCHIE: That's why I've come for you, Bev. That's why I come to take you back.

BEVERLEY: I can't . . .

ARCHIE: It's just what Vera was singin'. . . . *Today* is the great day. Today is the day to *make love.* Today is the day we live! Tomorrow is the mystery . . . perhaps the day we die! . . . Sing to us, Bev, will ya? (*Beverley laughs*) Sing to us. Give us a Vera.

BEVERLEY: Oh Artie, please . . . I feel so silly . . . tears on me cheek . . . so sentimental. . . . It's only that we've grown so old. It's only that life has passed us by. That's all that moves us to tears, really . . .

ARCHIE: Stop that! Life's not bloody passed us by, Beverley Leach! Life's just been waitin' in the rain. Somebody's pushed the bleedin' *pause button!* . . . But now we're *talkin'* ta one another, lovey, aren't we? And when lovers get ta talkin', anything's possible, isn't it? . . . Please, give us a Vera, Bev, will ya? (*Suddenly, Archie drops down on to bended knee*) You've got a man on his knee beggin' ya, Beverley! (*Beverley laughs*) Do it! Don't let the chance pass! It's the best of life for us, Bev. Do it, Bev.

(*Beverley sings, imitating Vera Lynn. Archie puts his head on her lap; listening lovingly. Beverley stops singing; looks at Archie, strokes his hair; speaks*)

BEVERLEY: I'm not Vera Lynn, Artie. I don't know quite who I am any more, but I do know I'm not her, not Vera.

ARCHIE: *I* know who you are: You're Beverley Leach, the woman I dearly love.

(*Archie kisses Beverley. It is a long, loving kiss.*

Cecily re-enters from kitchen with portable phone; sees them kiss)

CECILY: Oh, shit.

(*Cecily exits into the kitchen. Archie and Beverley take a giant step back from one another*)

BEVERLEY: This is awful!

ARCHIE: No, it's not awful, Bev. It's *gorgeous!*

(*Archie moves to kiss Beverley again. She pulls back quickly*)

BEVERLEY: Get away! Get back!

CECILY (*calling out loudly from off in the kitchen*): I'm done with my phone call! I'm coming back into the living room! You have been advised! (*Cecily re-enters; smiles*) Hi, y'all! What's up?

(*There is an embarrassed pause*)

BEVERLEY: I'm going to my room. I want to be left alone. (*To both, sternly*) I mean it!

(*Beverley exits upstairs. There is a pause. Archie looks at Cecily; smiles.*

Zelly enters from the kitchen. He is no longer wearing his stormcoat or boots. He seems to have been in the house a while. Archie's smile fades. Zelly stands staring at Archie silently)

ARCHIE: I thought you were out walking, Zelly.

ZELLY (*unrelenting stare*): I came back.

(*Cecily laughs nervously*)

CECILY: Hey, you guys probably wanna talk about things on your own, huh? . . . Undisturbed. I'll be in my room packing.

(Cecily gathers together her portable phone, cigarettes, work folders, scripts; exits upstairs.

Zelly continues staring at Archie)

ARCHIE: What are ya starin' at, mate?

ZELLY: It's time, Archie.

ARCHIE: Time for what? (*No reply. Zelly continues staring*) Time for what? (*No reply. Zelly continues staring. Archie shouts angrily*) *I've asked you a question!*

(No reply. Zelly continues staring. Archie meets Zelly's stare for a moment, but then loses courage; looks down. Zelly laughs. The lights fade to black.)

ACT TWO

Scene Two

Same day, two hours later.

In the darkness, we hear last moments of a recording of Vera Lynn singing "Yours."

Lights fade up in living room on Beverley, Zelly and Archie, listening to conclusion of song.

Beverley is absolutely silent at the window, looking outside. Zelly stands across the room, leaning against the bookcase. Archie sits in overstuffed chair, weeping, as he sings along with Vera.

We hear the scratch of needle against antique 78rpm record, still turning on turntable.

Zelly walks to phonograph, lifts arm.

ARCHIE: That's what she sang to me.

ZELLY: Those were different times, Archie. Couples, ya know, *got together* pretty easy. It woulda be'n hard to expect Beverley ta just stay, ya know, *yours*.

ARCHIE: I didn't find it hard to expect. I expected it. We had an agreement, Bev and me, didn't we?

ZELLY: Nobody knew from one day to the next whether we'd be alive. They were bringing in the dead and wounded. It got to ya, somethin' wickid. It changed the rules kinda thing.

ARCHIE: You knew she was engaged ta me, didn't ya?

ZELLY: I . . . I guess I did. But that sorta thing didn't mean much . . . not with truckloads of war-wounded comin' in . . . boxcars on trains fulla the dead. You'd meet a girl, you'd like each other, you'd fall into each other's arms. It wasn't like boys on the make, just scorin' . . . it was much more desperate than that.

ARCHIE: I were in the same war, weren't I? It weren't so bloody desperate for me. We had a job ta do and we were doin' it bloody well. What kept us goin', we Brits, was the love of our country and the love of our families . . . kiddies, if you had 'em . . . mums and dads . . . our women. Bev was mine and you bloody stole her, didn't ya? Makin' yourself exotic with your far-away stories . . . fishin' boats and this and that . . . half-Jewish/half-Portuguese with Italian snuck in. . . . That sort of exoticism gets an innocent English girl's head swimmin'. . . . She forgets herself, don't she? She falls right over backwards, don't she? . . . Arms and legs spread akimbo . . .

ZELLY: Jesus, Archie, this is *nuts!* We're talkin' something that happened almost fifty years ago!

ARCHIE: True love never dies.

ZELLY: Okay, okay, okay! It's out in the open. I stole Bev from you. Okay? Fine. So what's anybody s'pose ta do about any of this?

ARCHIE: You've had her for forty-five years. I want the rest.

ZELLY: What's this?

ARCHIE: I'm takin' her back with me!

ZELLY: What?

ARCHIE: What can't you comprehend here, Zelly? I'm speakin' the King's bloody English, aren't I? I'm takin' Beverley Leach home to England where she *belongs!* . . .

ZELLY: Read my lips. (*Points to lips; yells*) Over my dead fuckin' body!

ARCHIE: That may well be. The choice is the lady's, isn't it? (*Zelly and Archie turn and look at Beverley at the window. There is a moment's pause*) It's time, Bev. The moment of truth has come.

BEVERLEY (*calling offstage to Cecily*): Cecily, come down the stairs and into the room. Join us. There's no point in hearing this on the sly.

CECILY (*walking into view on the staircase*): Why does overhearing any conversation between your parents involving sex make you feel six years old and stupid? (*Goes to chair;*

sits) I'm sitting . . . I'm in the room . . . I'm one of the grown-ups . . . I'm really uncomfortable.

BEVERLEY: From the time Cecily was six until she was sixteen, I had a love affair with a local man.

ARCHIE: You what?

BEVERLEY: Be quiet, Arthur! It's my turn! . . . (*Pauses; composes herself*) He was married, two children. A boy and a girl. James and Judy. He was an accountant . . . not very exciting, but really very affectionate. (*Beverley moves to a position behind Cecily's chair; touches Cecily's hair*) Cecily knew about it. Children know everything that goes on in a house. (*Looks at Zelly*) Zelly knew about it, as well. Not every detail . . . but you knew, didn't you, darling? . . .

ZELLY: What's the point of this, huh? This isn't anybody's business . . .

BEVERLEY (*angrily*): The point is that I'm talking! . . . The point is that I'm speaking my thoughts! . . . I'm choosing my words! *Now, be quiet!* (*There is a pause*) When Cecily was young, there was no end to Zelly's old girlfriends traipsing through this house. The one who cleaned for us . . . what's-her-name? . . . Shoes . . .

ZELLY: Bootsie.

BEVERLEY: Exactly. Bootsie. And the babysitter with the enormous bottom . . . ginger-haired, Irish . . .

ZELLY: Mary-Louise?

BEVERLEY: Mary-Louise.

CECILY: I remember Mary-Louise. I *loathed* Mary-Louise. She smelled bad.

BEVERLEY: Zelly used to kiss Mary-Louise hello and goodbye . . . on the mouth.

ZELLY: Mary-Louise was like a cousin.

BEVERLEY: You have Irish cousins?

ZELLY: I said *like* a cousin!

BEVERLEY: What about the Ciolino girl?

ZELLY: It wasn't the same thing! They all lived here! They were all local people! None of 'em traveled thousands of goddam miles to get here like this Archie Bennett person. I may not know much, but I know men! No man comes halfway around the world for a bowl a' shrimpy chowder! . . .

BEVERLEY: Oh, I see. It's the mileage that determines the severity of the threat. It's a small point, but England's not "halfway around the world" from here, darling. It's only three thousand miles . . .

ZELLY: Fine.

BEVERLEY: I think it's charming that you feel so threatened, dear. (*Pauses*) Zelly had a string of extra women in his life. I just had the one extra man: Allen. Allen loved me. We met in Allen's office Tuesdays and Fridays, from three til five, whilst Cecily had her piano lesson. Cecily learned Chopin's body of work and I learned Allen's body.

ARCHIE: Bloody hell! (*Cecily laughs*) And where's he, now, then, this accountant?

BEVERLEY: Gone . . . dead. He wasn't young, not even then. (*Beverley touches Cecily's cheek*) Poor Cecily's seen it all, haven't you, dear?

ARCHIE: Whatchu mean "Cecily's seen it all"? Was she bloody in the room wi' yas?

BEVERLEY (*imitating Archie's North country accent*): No, she weren't, mate! Not wi' Allen, but she were bloody in the room wi' me and Zelly, sluggin' it out.

ARCHIE: Zelly struck ya?

BEVERLEY: Jesus! Belt up, will ya, man?! Ya go on like an bloody *ignorant!* (*Pauses; her "Americanized" accent returns*) Growing up with parents in a loveless marriage is a *disaster!* . . . I was too selfish to see it at the time for what it was, but I see it clearly now. I've never talked with Cecily, mother to child . . . *woman to woman* . . . not once, not ever before now . . . but I am now . . . I am talking. (*Pauses*) I'm sorry, Cecily. I apologize for not making a good marriage. I know you're unhappy and I know why. I take full responsibility for my part in it.

CECILY: It's not all your fault, Mother. Don't think it is.

BEVERLEY: I don't. I know it's not all my fault. But a great deal of it is: my fault. And I'm sorry for all that. I love you, Cecily.

CECILY: I love you, too.

(*Cecily weeps; then, laughs; then, turns to Zelly, drying her eyes*)

CECILY: I've asked Mum to come out to California with me . . . to live with me.

ZELLY: Your mother lives here . . . with her husband: with *me!* (*To Beverley; angrily*) These things are in the past, lady! These things are forgiven and forgotten.

BEVERLEY: Zelly's got another family.

ZELLY: Jesus, Bev!

(*Zelly goes to window, looks outside, his back now turned to Beverley and others*)

BEVERLEY: He got a young Italian girl pregnant . . . about ten years into our marriage. I was nearly thirty. Cecily was five. The girl was twenty. She and her mother worked for Zelly, cutting fish on the line. The mother knew about it . . . about what was goin' on with her daughter and Zelly. In fact, she almost seemed to *approve!* . . . I knew the girl myself, of course. She wasn't beautiful, but she was what you'd call *good-looking*—dark-eyed, round-faced, large-breasted, strong. (*Pauses*) I didn't know what to do. I didn't want to go home . . . to England . . . My dad worshipped Zelly and my mother would never take my part against him. Being so deeply unhappy in my marriage somehow made me feel *stupid.* (*Pauses*) She had his child. Everybody in Gloucester knew about it . . . my friends, Cecily's friends. . . . And everybody knew we knew, as well. Nobody ever said a word about any of it to us *directly* . . . but couldn't you bloody hear the hushed whispers, the snide comments? How superior it made them all feel! . . . In this house, it was always the *unspeakable!* Zelly never let us talk about it, never let me bring it up. And I agreed with him somehow. It was never spoken of out loud, until now. (*Pauses*) She never married: the girl, I mean, not the child. He did: the child. He married and moved away. He writes to Zelly from time to time, doesn't he, dear? He calls him "Dad." The girl's still in town. She's how old, now? Fifty-five? This all still hurts me, Zelly. (*Pauses*) When you're young, you trust in people . . . in marriage. . . . Marriage seems . . . possible . . . natural. (*Wipes her eyes; smiles*) There are so many secrets in a marriage, aren't there? So many lies. But at the end of the day, all the empty excitement of love affairs and heart-pounding intrigue can't distract any of us from our essential unhappiness. I am a profoundly unhappy woman. I've been this for an unthinkable number of years now. (*Pauses*) That's everybody's Big Secret, really, isn't it? Profound unhappiness . . . lack of purpose . . . lack of reason. I'm unhappy, Cecily's unhappy, Zelly's unhappy and, Arthur, you're a *misery!* Take my word for it! (*Pauses*) There was only one thrilling time in my entire life, Arthur. I was seventeen years old and bombs were falling all around me. Up the road a mile or so from my house, there was this RAF base with about two thousand lads mostly my age . . . you, Arthur, and nineteen hundred and ninety-nine others, all young, all beautiful to look at, all gorgeous to the touch, all scared to death to live or die. Up the road three miles or so, there was Zelly's American air base with about a thousand more lads, same age, same life. All told, there couldn't've been more than a hundred unmarried girls my age in the entire area. Bombs falling from the sky almost every night of our lives and a ratio of thirty lads to every one of us young girls. Now, this, for me, *defines* thrilling! (*Pauses*) Our parents were telling us to stay away from the flyboys, but our hearts and our minds and our bodies were saying, "Live for the moment, girl! Any one of Hitler's bombs could be the one with your name on it! Don't die unfulfilled! Don't die *unloved!* Don't die . . . *untouched!*" Don't talk to me about "a thrilling life," Arthur. I have known the ultimate thrill of my particular life and only a fool would imagine such a thrill could be challenged or equalled . . . or recaptured. (*Pauses*) For me, there have been very few discernable advantages to peacetime. My needs were always so different from Zelly's. He just needed a few chaps to remind him that he was once a hero. What I needed, quite honestly, was thirty men fighting over me. I needed to be young and beautiful, walking through tiny cobbled streets lined with hungry young men, all wanting me . . . all staring at my breasts and my bottom . . . touchin' me with their eyes . . . wanting me. I did need that. And, I'm afraid, I still bloody do. I had that. And anything less was and is . . . sadly lacking. (*Pauses*) Isn't it awful to hear this said out loud? (*Pauses*) It was, I admit, quite exciting when I knew that Zelly was actually cheating on me. It gave me a kind of freedom. I knew I could do whatever I wanted with whomever I wanted . . . and I couldn't ever be blamed for me sins! . . . (*Pauses*) Isn't it awful to hear this said out loud? (*Pauses*) But in the end, between us, between Zelly and me, it was dead. It felt like I was trapped in a cave alone . . . only I wasn't alone, was I? I was just bloody . . . *trapped.* (*Laughs; then*) Don't you think that people like us finally die because they want to? I do.

ARCHIE: Think that?

BEVERLEY: Want to die.

CECILY: Don't say that, Mum . . . please.

ARCHIE: Sod that, woman! You're talkin' like a right nutter! What's ahead is The Big Sleep! No bloody more, no bloody less! You don't need rest, lady, as you've done nothin' to tire you out! Fancy you callin' me "a misery" and "an ignorant," when you're talkin' like a *pathetic spot!* Get off your bottom, Beverley! Life's precious! If you've missed the point, I'll give it ya!

(*Archie grabs Beverley; kisses her. Beverley breaks from the kiss; slaps Archie's face sharply. It is a stunning blow*)

BEVERLEY: Don't you dare! I'll decide who I kiss and when.

ARCHIE (*holding his cheek*): That really hurt.

BEVERLEY: Come here! (*Beverley pulls Archie to her; kisses him. Zelly watches helplessly. Beverley breaks the kiss; looks at Zelly*) Do you want a kiss, Zelly? (*Zelly moans a "yes;" Beverley giggles*) Where am I getting this girlish *power?* . . . Come here, Zelly.

(*Zelly and Beverley kiss. Archie stares helplessly*)

ARCHIE: I don't like this.

(*He makes a move toward Zelly and Beverley. Cecily suddenly steps in, interrupts Archie*)

CECILY: *Don't!*

ARCHIE: Or what, Suzie? (*Archie is enraged; pulls Beverley away from Zelly. A confession flies from his lips*) I wish to God I had been the one who had you in my sights, 'steada the Jerry! I never would've botched it, believe you me!

ZELLY (*stunned*): *What?*

ARCHIE: You heard me! It's me life's one and only great regret. I was up there in the same bloody skirmish. If I'd a' had my sights on you, I wouldn't a' bloody missed. I would've made a corpse of you! The Jerry made a bloody *hero* of you instead. It's the only reason she married you, mate. She told me that herself. You can thank bloody Adolph for your marriage!

ZELLY: I should fuckin' kill you!

ARCHIE: You and what fuckin' brigade?!

(*Zelly stares at Beverley*)

ZELLY: You told him this, Beverley? (*Beverley looks at Zelly, then looks down*) Is this why you married me? . . . Because of some cowboy-flyboy heroics?

BEVERLEY (*after a pause*): No.

ZELLY: Then why did ya?

BEVERLEY: I married you because I loved you . . . because I wanted to be your wife.

ZELLY: And now?

(*Archie giggles*)

BEVERLEY (*holding back tears*): Please don't, Zelly.

ZELLY: I don't hear an answer to my question.

ARCHIE: Answer the man, Bev.

BEVERLEY: What's your question, Zelly?

ZELLY: Now: would you marry me now?

BEVERLEY: Don't do this, Zelly.

ZELLY (*yelling roughly*): *Answer me, goddammit!*

BEVERLEY: No. I wouldn't marry you now, Zelly. No.

(*Archie giggles*)

BEVERLEY: I won't ask the same question of you, Zelly, because I know the answer.

ZELLY: We don't get this time back, lady! It's *gone!* It's . . .

(*Zelly turns away; suddenly, he weeps*)

ARCHIE: I spent a bloody bomb on this trip and it was worth it. Twice the cost would've been worth it! This is a dream come true! (*Zelly punches Archie*) You struck me!

ZELLY: That's the way us Yanks do it, *mate!*

ARCHIE: I'll show you the way a Yorkshireman does it, *bub!*

(*Archie and Zelly have a fistfight. As they are both rather old, it is a slow and careful fistfight. First, Archie hits Zelly, then Zelly hits Archie. And so it goes. In the end, Zelly runs Archie to the door*)

ARCHIE: Hey! Hey!

(*Zelly opens the front door; shoves Archie outside; closes the door, locks it; faces Beverley*)

ZELLY: I would so marry you now, Beverley. I would so! I swear ta God I would!

(*We see Archie outside window, shivering*)

BEVERLEY: No you wouldn't, Zelly! Don't lie to me! I know you too well. Don't lie to me. Don't lie to *yourself!*

(*The doorbell chimes*)

ZELLY: Stay with me, Beverley. I know I haven't been much of a husband, but I can be . . . I will be. Give me a chance, Bev, please . . . I'm begging you. (*Sees Beverley laugh*) What the hell is funny?

BEVERLEY: Your telling me that you "haven't been much of a husband for forty-five years," but now you want "a chance"! A *chance?* You don't think that's *funny?*

(*Doorbell chimes again. We see Archie running from window to window, shivering with the cold*)

BEVERLEY: I'm going to my room to pack my things. It's over, Zelly. Don't blame Cecily for my leavin' but, I must admit, it was she who finally got me off my bottom by telling me her biggest fear was that she might turn out to be just like me. That was my biggest fear as well: That I'd turn out to be just like my mother. Not my mother fully . . . just my mother *married.* (*Pauses*) I wasn't strong enough for any of us, was I? . . . But now I will be. I'm leavin', Zelly. It's over. (*The doorbell chimes again*) Let Arthur back in, please, dear. He's an old man. He'll die out there.

(Zelly sobs. Beverley goes to him, takes his hand, brings his hand to her lips; kisses his hand in an almost gentlemanly fashion)

BEVERLEY: I'm not going with you, Cecily. That's your life, not mine! . . . I'm going to pack.

(Beverley exits up staircase.

There is a moment's pause. Then, the doorbell chimes, again. The lights fade out.)

ACT TWO

Scene Three

Late afternoon, same day.

In darkness, we hear Chopin being played on the Hammond organ lightly.

Lights up in living room on Zelly, Cecily and Archie. Cecily sits at the Hammond organ, playing a Chopin étude . . . and playing it well. Archie wears his overcoat. He paces from wall to wall. Zelly stands at window, looking out. Archie's and Cecily's suitcases are in evidence near front door. We hear tea kettle's whistle off.

CECILY: I'll get it. *(Cecily exits into kitchen)*

ARCHIE: If she'd have been my wife, I wouldn't've let her go, I can tell you that!

(Zelly doesn't reply. Archie looks at his watch; paces to front door; returns to living room)

ARCHIE: Nothin' but broken homes out there! All over the world, "Family" means bloody nothin'. I read the papers! I see the bloody television! Divorce, divorce, divorce! People sayin' the til-death-do-us-part part with one foot out the bloody door! (*To Zelly, angrily*) Can't you control your own wife, for God's sake, man?! Can't you show the woman earthly *reason?!* . . . Bloody war-hero, me arse! I know a man when I see one and I see bloody *none!*

(*Archie paces to the front door again; looks at his watch again*)

ARCHIE: If I miss this bloody train ta Boston, I'll miss me bloody boat back to England. And then what? I'll bloody tell ya what! I be stranded! I'll be one of the bloody hundred thousand homeless beggars I stepped over since I've been in bloody America! If I'm gonna be down and out, I'm gonna be down and out in bloody England where they know how ta make a chip butty and a decent cuppa tea!

CECILY (*entering with tea tray*): Tea's up, lads!

ARCHIE: How come you're so cheery, dearie?

CECILY (*North Country accent*): I'm bloody happy for me mum, mate! . . . That's what. Ready for a fresh cuppa?

ARCHIE: Give us one, then . . .

CECILY (*spooning sugar*): Was it two?

ARCHIE: Two.

CECILY (*hands cup to Archie*): Here ya are, love.

ARCHIE: Tar very much, lovey.

(*Archie sips his tea; winces*)

ARCHIE: Gawww! What's this?

CECILY: It's herbal. Better for you than caffeine when you're traveling.

ARCHIE: What *is* this stuff?

CECILY: Rose hips.

ARCHIE: Rose hips? Sounds like the name of a bloody exotic dancer! . . . (*Car horn sounds; off*) That's me. It's me taxi. (*Archie goes out front door, leaving suitcase outside; yells to taxi driver*) Won't be a minute! (*Archie re-enters; goes to Zelly, extends his hand for handshake*) All's fair in love and war, mate. (*They shake hands*) Thanks for lettin' me stay in your house, Zelly. We're the lucky ones, ya know. We're the survivors. We've still got life ta live. (*Pauses*) Maybe we'll see each other again . . . I expect we will . . . don't know where, don't know when . . . (*Smiles*) Vera. (*Pauses*) God bless, Zelly. (*To Cecily*) Oh, Cecily, love, a Dr. Weingarten called, whilst you were up talkin' with your mum. I told him he was doin' a shitty job and that you'd committed suicide. Let's give *him* somethin' ta worry about, eh, lovey? (*Goes to door; opens it, stands poised with suitcases*) Take care of yourselves. If you don't, no one else will.

(*Archie exits the play. After a pause, Cecily goes to Zelly with a cup of tea*)

CECILY: Here. This one's real tea. I made his cup up special.

ZELLY (*smiling; taking cup*): Thanks.

CECILY: You're welcome.

(*Zelly looks at it; sighs; looks at Cecily*)

ZELLY: You're gonna hav'ta help me through this, Cecie. I can't face this alone.

CECILY: You want me to stay awhile?

ZELLY: Could you? . . . Would you?

CECILY: Yes.

(*Zelly reaches out his hand to Cecily. She takes it, holds her father's hand*)

ZELLY: You think she'll come back?

CECILY: It's up to her, isn't it?

ZELLY: It can't end this way. Women can't just leave.

(*Lights crossfade to spotlight on Beverley downstage, facing Zelly and Cecily, speaking words from a letter she has written to Zelly*)

BEVERLEY: Dear Zelly. The oddness of being so far from you is indescribable. (*Pauses*) I know it's unfair, my being the one to leave. The one who stays behind feels the loser somehow. I know this is true because I so often thought you'd leave *me* . . . (*Pauses*) I never imagined I'd be the one . . . the one to leave. It doesn't seem like me, does it? (*Spotlight fades up on Zelly downstage. He holds Beverley's pink letter in his hand. Beverley continues speaking the words of her letter aloud*) Don't worry about me. I'm in a safe place. I'd like to tell you where I am, but I don't yet dare. I'm frightened you'll come after me, force me back. That wouldn't be good. I've spent much too much time in my married life planning what I would do after you died. Those were my secret fantasies, Zelly . . . the things I would do after you were gone. I never wanted you dead. I just wanted to leave and I could never imagine any other way out the door. (*Pauses*) I have a chance to substitute-teach, Zelly. Two days a week. I know it doesn't sound earth-shattering news, but it's the most exciting thing that's happened to me in my life in the past thirty years! (*Pauses*) It must be terrible for you to read this. (*Pauses*) You are so present in my life, Zelly. Even though the thought of being near you fills me with dread, still and all, whatever I see, I think immediately that I should rush to tell you about it. (*Pauses*) After my dad died, when I went to see my mum, I remember how lost she seemed without her "darlin' husbin' Den." . . . She told me that the first thought she'd had after she knew for sure Dad was dead was, "I can hardly wait to ring Den up and tell him who died!" (*Pauses*) I could hardly wait to write this letter to you, Zelly, because I could hardly wait to tell you the most amazing news: Beverley's left Zelly! (*Pauses*) I'll write to you, again, soon . . . Yours, as never before . . . Bev.

(*Lights fade out on Zelly. Beat. Then, lights fade out on Beverley.*

Music in: Vera Lynn "Yours." The play is over.)